W9-AMU-595

THE
COMPLETE
DOG
TRAINING
MANUAL

BRUCE FOGLE, D.V.M.

Training sequences by
PATRICIA HOLDEN WHITE

RD
PRESS

MONTREAL

PROJECT EDITOR
Tracey Williams

ART EDITOR
Tim Scott

MANAGING EDITOR
Krystyna Mayer

MANAGING ART EDITOR
Derek Coombes

U.S. EDITOR
Mary Ann Lynch

ASPCA CONSULTANTS
Stephen Zawistowski, PhD
Jacque Lynn Schultz
Elizabeth Teal

DTP DESIGNER
Doug Miller

PRODUCTION CONTROLLER
Antony Heller

TRAINER
Patricia Holden White

A DORLING KINDERSLEY BOOK

Published in Canada in 1994 by
The Reader's Digest Association (Canada) Ltd.
215 Redfern Avenue, Westmount, Quebec H3Z 2V9

The Reader's Digest Association (Canada) Ltd.
is a licensed user of the trademark RD Press

First published in Great Britain in 1994
by Dorling Kindersley Limited,
9 Henrietta Street, London WC2E 8PS

Copyright © 1994 Dorling Kindersley Limited, London
Text copyright © 1994 Bruce Fogle

All rights reserved. No part of this publication may
be reproduced, stored in a retrieval system, or transmitted
in any form or by any means, electronic, mechanical,
photocopying, recording or otherwise, without the prior
written permission of the copyright owner.

CANADIAN CATALOGUING IN PUBLICATION DATA

Fogle, Bruce.
    The complete dog training manual

1st Canadian ed.
Includes index.
ISBN 0-88850-313-X

    1. Dogs – Training. I. Reader's Digest
Association (Canada). II. Title.

SF431.F64 1994   636.7'0887   C93-090674-8

Color reproduced by Colourscan, Singapore
Printed and bound by Mondadori, Italy

94 95 96 97 / 5 4 3 2 1

Contents

Introduction

The dog evolved from its wolf ancestors over 10,000 years ago, and since that time it has lived and worked with humans. The natural inclinations of the wolf were exaggerated through controlled breeding, and lines of dogs evolved bearing distinct abilities. Breeds were created for specific purposes, such as hunting, herding flocks of livestock, guarding campsites, and fighting by our sides during battle.

Canine evolution

In all regions of the northern hemisphere – the natural territory of the wolf – our distant relatives tamed the wolf and through controlled breeding produced the dog. In North America, the Inuit created sled dogs, animals with powerful shoulders who were willing to pull heavy loads. In Asia, a variety of dogs emerged, ranging in size from heavy-boned war dogs like Mastiffs, to delicate companion dogs such as the Pekingese. Dogs with the ability to run swiftly were bred to chase game, thereby creating the root stock of the modern-day Afghan, Saluki, and Greyhound.

Speciality breeds

Farther south in Asia, smaller hunting dogs evolved: the Singing Dog and the Dingo. These animals accompanied the Aboriginals when they settled in Papua New Guinea and Australia. In Europe, too, the wolf was tamed. The spitz-type dogs of northern Europe served our ancestors' needs by chasing large game. Speciality hunting breeds emerged, such as the Elkhound, Deerhound, Irish Wolfhound, and Otter Hound. Coursing and digging dogs – experts at killing small animals – were bred selectively, and today's terriers are their descendants. In Africa, Basenjis evolved as silent hunting companions.

Breeding the domestic dog

Generations of selective breeding resulted in dogs becoming even more specialized in their abilities to work for or with humans. Some scenting dogs were developed to follow air scent, and others to follow ground scent. Dogs were bred to fight with bears, bulls, or each other, for our amusement. With the invention of the gun came the emergence of sporting dogs. These canines would point to, flush out, or retrieve game.

Canine companions

The role of the dog is still evolving, and many former canine roles have been lost. However, with the emergence of Kennel Clubs throughout the world during the last century, over 400 breeds of dog – each developed for a specific purpose – still exist. Today, most of these dogs serve a single purpose, that of companions to humans.

Problems of contemporary canines

Dogs were bred to work, to use their mental and physical energy, and to concentrate and be alert. However, many modern-day canines, although fed regularly, kept physically healthy, and protected from danger, really lead very boring lives.

Leading a dull life

One of the consequences of this dull lifestyle is the development of behavioral problems. Neighbors complain because dogs howl. Owners find exercising their dogs frustrating because their pet persistently pulls on the lead, tries to attack other dogs, or chases cyclists. People who do not own dogs often find them – and their owners – unpleasant because owners let their dogs soil public places. These problems are not the dog's fault; they are our fault simply because we have not trained our pets properly.

Canine euthanasia

One of the most disturbing statistics in veterinary medicine concerns the cause of death of dogs. In many regions of the world, the most common cause of death of dogs under 18 months old is not illness, disease or injury, but euthanasia. One common reason why owners decide that their dog should die is that the dog has a behavioral problem. Although

specific breeds are associated with certain types of behavior, most behavioral problems develop as a consequence of inadequate training.

Training your dog

Dog training is neither a contest to see who is most powerful, nor an ego-boosting exercise. It is never necessary to use violence. It is, however, essential to use common sense, be lavish with rewards, and have fun. Good training is based upon mutual trust and respect.

Learning to train

Certain instincts and behaviors have been exaggerated in some breeds. However, regardless of breed, each dog has its own personality, and the amount of training that is necessary varies with the individual. How your dog thinks is described in Chapter One. Training does not mean enrolling in weekly classes, although with good instruction, classes are an excellent way of teaching you how to train your dog. Training does not mean a daily trudge to a nearby park or field to put your dog through a series of exercises. Training is an attitude as much as an exercise. In Chapter One you will also learn how to use rewards and give commands and, most important of all, how to time your commands, rewards, and discipline properly.

Early training

Chapter Two contains information on puppy training, including the value of crate training and house training, the importance of grooming, and basic obedience commands. It also gives advice on the kinds of equipment to use. By following these instructions you will give your dog an advantage in life, and increase the likelihood that for the next 10 to 15 years you will have a perfect canine companion.

Personal training

More advanced training is discussed in Chapter Three. Each training exercise includes detailed instructions, illustrated with step-by-step photographs. Every dog is an individual. In varying degrees, each is interested in mental and physical stimulation, sex, guarding territory, eating, sleeping, and personal comfort. Its temperament, attention span, age, and sex influence its propensity towards training. Not all dogs respond to the same teaching methods, and training techniques sometimes need to be altered to suit the individual's personality. Just as training follows set patterns, problems follow set patterns, and information on training dogs with different needs is included. As well as advising on basic obedience training, Chapter Three includes information on training your dog to hold, retrieve, speak, and use its paw. Introducing your dog to children, strangers, other dogs, and other animals is also discussed.

Canine behavioral problems

Even with conscientious training, some dogs still develop bad habits or behavioral problems; these are dealt with in Chapter Four. This chapter includes a discussion on the difference between natural dog behaviors that humans find unacceptable, such as scent marking, and learned bad habits, such as destroying homes when they are left alone.

Causes and cures

Common canine bad habits, and advice on how to deal with them, are comprehensively covered in Chapter Four. The causes and cures of behavioral disorders such as pulling on the lead, not coming when called, chasing, different forms of aggression, nervousness and fear biting, car and sex problems, boredom, and eating difficulties are described. This chapter also contains advice on where to obtain information on more specialized training.

Commitment is rewarding

It is not necessary to be a brilliant trainer to produce a well-mannered dog, but you must be committed to the task. Training involves making decisions about where your dog sleeps, what kind of toys it plays with, and when it is fed, as well as teaching basic commands. Training encourages your dog's natural skills, reinforces your status as leader, and teaches you how to understand your dog. Once you have achieved this understanding, you will discover that no other domesticated animal offers such active and rewarding companionship.

CHAPTER ONE

Your Dog's Mind

Dogs are similar to humans in that they need both companionship and mental and physical stimulation to achieve their potential. They respond well to rewards and develop bad habits when they are bored. They are always learning, whether they are being "schooled" or not. However, dogs are not people in disguise. Every dog has its own unique personality, and intelligence, tolerance, and trainability vary with each individual. Through selective breeding, humans have accentuated some of the wolf's personality traits in some dogs and reduced others. Overall, the canine is our best animal friend because it is so willing to live within a human "pack" and communicate with us.

How Your Dog Thinks

Your dog thinks in a very logical way, but canine logic is simpler than human logic. Like their wolf ancestors, dogs are pack animals. They respect and respond to their pack leader and are primarily interested in survival and comfort. To a dog, survival means food. This is advantageous during training, because it means that tasty food snacks can be used as potent rewards for your dog's good behavior. You can also incorporate the dog's natural desires to seek comfort, to play, and to have its own personal space into your training routine as rewards for its responsive behavior.

Original dog pack

The domestic dog's behavior corresponds to that of the wolf. Through selective breeding, humans have accentuated certain wolf behaviors and reduced others. Regardless of size or conformation, your dog retains the wolf heritage.

Modern dog pack

Pet dogs rarely have the opportunity to act as a true pack. Sled dogs are an exception, but here there are two pack leaders – one canine and one human.

Food is given to canine pack leader

Dog pack leader shows authority by rising above other dogs

Willing to obey

Few dogs want to be pack leaders. The vast majority feel safe, secure, and content knowing that there is someone in command. Early obedience training reinforces this natural behavior and teaches puppies to respond to commands given by humans.

Puppy receives reward for obeying command

Survival techniques

Dogs are always learning, and their mental and physical activities are geared to survival. Rewarding action such as scavenging will cause it to increase unless you intervene and stop the behavior.

Dog leans against its pack leader for security and comfort

Physical Aspects

SMALL DOGS

From birth, large dogs require more food, so it is an effective reward. Smaller dogs require less food, so it may be a less powerful reward. Small breeds are often more selective eaters than large ones, so you may need to find some especially tempting treat to use as a training reward. Chopped-up hot dogs or cheese generally works.

Comfort seekers

Like humans, dogs enjoy the comforts of life. If you let a young puppy sit on the furniture in your home, it will always think it is allowed to sit there. You can avoid this problem by providing your dog with its own comfortable, personal space.

Avoiding discomfort

It is rarely necessary to physically discipline a dog. Most dogs learn to change their ways to avoid milder indirect discipline, such as a squirt from a water pistol.

Dense coat prevents loss of body heat

COAT DENSITY

Many dogs seek human contact for comfort, but breeds with dense coats can appear more independent than those with thin coats, preferring solitude simply because it is cooler.

Personal space

Like wolves, dogs instinctively defend their pack's territory. Pet dogs learn to recognize the perimeters of their human family's territory, whether it is the car, the home, or the garden, and will often defend it.

Mental stimulation

Dogs need mental as well as physical stimulation. Providing your dog with a small selection of unique toys to play with teaches it to chew only certain items.

Social gatherings

Make sure that your puppy is properly socialized with other canines when it is young. If it is not, it may feel secure only with human companions when it matures.

Rewarding good behavior

Always reward good behavior, but do not expect your dog to respond the first time you issue a command. However, dogs soon learn to associate certain words with specific reactions and rewards.

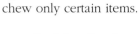

Dog returns for its favorite toy

Breed Differences

For at least 10,000 years, humans have been involved in dog breeding. Dogs were originally bred for their behaviors and abilities. It is only in the last 200 years that they have been bred primarily for size, coat, and color. By originally being bred for temperament, certain body shapes and coat densities were also selected. In perpetuating those characteristics, humans have also perpetuated breed differences in behavior. Specific breeds are associated with certain aspects of behavior, and some types of dogs are more predisposed toward training than others.

Heavy bone structure provides anchorage for powerful muscles

Herding breeds

Collies, shepherd dogs, and cattle dogs evolved to work as teams with shepherds and farmers. Originally bred for their stamina and to nip at the heels of livestock, they are loyal and energetic dogs. They bark when they are excited and have a tendency to nip.

Selective breeding has resulted in dense coat

Northern breeds

The Nordic or spitz group of dogs includes the Husky, Elkhound, Japanese Akita, and Chow Chow. These dogs have powerful shoulders and dense coats, which they shed abundantly. They have tremendous stamina and are quite independent and aloof.

Guarding dogs

Mountain dogs such as the Bernese and Great Pyrenees were bred to guard flocks of sheep in the absence of the shepherd. They are relaxed but independent canines, with a tendency to be overprotective. Breeds such as Dobermanns and Boxers were bred for protection.

Sight hounds

Greyhounds, Whippets, Deerhounds, Afghan Hounds, and Salukis are all built for speed. Sometimes aloof and distant, sight hounds are not overwhelmingly demonstrative dogs.

Sporting dogs

Setters, pointers, spaniels, and especially retrievers, were all bred to be cooperative and to respond to human commands. As a result, they are often particularly affectionate dogs.

Sex Differences

In the same way that different breeds of dog have certain personality profiles, the different sexes have traits peculiar to them.

The male dog's brain is "masculinized" by a surge of hormone just before it is born. That is why even before puberty, males tend to grow bigger and behave in the classically masculine ways of being territorial and dominant. At puberty, and again at around two years of age, masculine behavior can become exaggerated – often making training difficult.

The female dog's brain is "neutral" at birth and becomes "feminized" at puberty. Female hormones can increase possessive behavior and can alter mood, change taste buds, and increase the dog's need to den. Neutering just before sexual maturity often guarantees that your dog's existing personality will be perpetuated.

Scent hounds

Bloodhounds, Basset Hounds, and Beagles were originally bred to follow scent, work in packs, and howl signals to their masters. They communicate well with other dogs and are able to follow the weakest trails.

Nose is large to capture scent

Terriers

Originally developed to chase small game and vermin, most terriers are small, robust diggers with powerful barks. They rarely back down when challenged and are the breeds most likely to snap and nip.

Companion dogs

Toy dogs such as Chihuahuas, Tibetan breeds, small poodles and spaniels, and bichons have always been bred for companionship. They thrive on affection and human contact.

Coat needs frequent attention to prevent matting

Personality Types

Although each breed of dog has its own general personality profile, ultimately every dog is unique. While some dogs are extroverts and like to be the center of attention, others are more submissive. Both types of dogs can be trained well, but different approaches are needed. Where your dog has come from and what it has experienced early in life will also affect its ability to be trained, as will its sex. Neutered dogs and females between seasons are easiest to train, while unneutered male dogs are the least responsive.

DIFFERENT PERSONALITIES

Dominant and confident
Some dogs, regardless of breed, have naturally confident personalities. Male dogs tend to be more dominant and confident than females. The dominant dog is most likely to resist training.

Submissive and insecure
Dogs with submissive personalities can be overwhelmed when commanded to obey. These dogs require a slow and gentle approach during training, so you should not issue commands too harshly.

Dog cowers fearfully

Easily distracted
Some dogs are more interested in playing with other dogs than in obeying their owners. Often these dogs were not properly socialized with people when they were puppies. It is best to train this type of dog on its own at first, rather than in a class.

Owner issues command

Cooperative and responsive
The dogs that are easiest to train are those that have natural curiosity and an affinity with humans. Dogs that explore and listen when spoken to respond most quickly to training.

Dog concentrates on another dog

SOURCES OF DOGS

Adopted dogs

Adopting a dog from a shelter can be a rewarding experience. Be sure first to find out all you can about the dog's behavior and be prepared to deal with any special needs.

Pet stores

Although many delightful dogs come through animal dealers, there is a greater likelihood of both disease and behavioral problems being present in these dogs than in those from more reliable sources. Many of these problems are created by inadequate socialization during the critical early months of the dog's life. Lack of human contact, isolation, and unpleasant incidents with other dogs all affect a dog's eventual behavior.

Responsible breeders

If you are interested in a pure breed, visit the breeder and ask to see the mother of the puppies and other adult dogs. A responsible breeder looks after the physical and psychological health of her dogs.

Personality Traits

DOMINANCE

Some dogs are extremely dominant and display their dominance by using intimidating body language, staring, holding their tail high, and even baring their teeth and barking in a threatening way. When training a dog with this type of personality, you should definitely seek professional help.

SUBMISSION

At the other end of the personality scale are dogs that are intensely submissive. They avoid eye contact, tuck their tails between their legs when their owner issues a command, and collapse in fear when anyone approaches them. If your dog behaves in this way, and if you have never trained a dog before, consider seeking professional help.

COMPROMISE

The vast majority of dogs are neither dominant nor submissive. In some circumstances and with some individuals they are dominant, and in other circumstances or with other individuals they are submissive. Most dogs have a mixture of both behaviors in their personalities.

MANIPULATION

Some dogs cleverly dominate their owners by claiming to be helpless and submissive. A dog that does this may scratch at its owner's legs and demand to be picked up or refuse to eat its food. These manipulators are dominant individuals that have learned different methods of showing authority.

PECKING ORDER

In a household, the pet dog should learn that it must obey all human members of its family. It should understand that under some circumstances, for example, when it hears a noise outside the window, it may express its natural dominance by barking a warning. In other circumstances, for example, when a human member of the household gives a command, it must obey.

Early Learning

By the time you acquire your dog, its behavior will have been influenced by its mother and by its relationship with its littermates. For example, if a mother barks to attract attention, her puppies are likely to behave in the same way. Experiences that occur between three and twelve weeks of age are critical in the development of a dog's personality. The best time to acquire a puppy is when it is about eight weeks old. By ensuring that it gains as much varied experience as possible during the following month, you will lay the groundwork for easy, productive, and rewarding training.

Puppy fearlessly examines new faces

Meeting people

Make sure that the new puppy meets as many people as possible while it is still very young. Unless your vet advises against it, take the puppy in the car, to work, and to friends' homes whenever possible. Let the puppy play with dogs that you know are healthy and introduce it to children and other adults.

Personal investigation

Playing with toys will provide the puppy with mental and physical stimulation. Find out which toys the puppy prefers (making sure that they are unlike other domestic articles), and use them as rewards during training.

Puppy eagerly takes part in play activity

Play constructively

You can play active games with the puppy, but you should always be in control of these. While you play, watch the puppy's behavior, and if it is about to sit, issue a "Sit" command.

Give immediate rewards

When the puppy obeys a command, offer an immediate reward, such as stroking or soothing words. As the dominant member of the partnership, you should always be in control.

Puppy enjoys being stroked

Early habits endure

If you carry a puppy constantly when it is very young, it will expect similar treatment when it feels insecure as an adult.

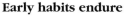

Give mental stimulation

Puppies that are actively stimulated at between three and twelve weeks of age grow into adults that are adept at both learning and problem solving. A puppy learns best by observing its mother's behavior. Within a human family, one person should be the "mother substitute" and be responsible for training the puppy, although all other family members should participate.

Social Development

SOCIAL GATHERINGS

Dogs must learn to behave properly, both with their own species and with others, especially humans. This is a difficult task, and the best time for them to learn is when they are very young – under four months old. Whenever possible, make sure that the puppy meets other species such as cats and horses when it is very young. Early socialization to other species reduces the likelihood of future problems. With the advice of your vet or local dog training club, organize or participate in supervised weekly puppy evenings *(see page 122)*. At these gatherings, puppies learn how to respond to other dogs and to strangers.

SOCIAL DEPRIVATION

Dogs that lack early social experiences can be difficult to train. Restricted contact with humans during puppyhood can limit the dog's ability to obey commands. Before acquiring a dog, find out as much as possible about its early experiences. The more a puppy has been handled, the more likely it is to respond to training. Puppies raised in cages in puppy mills can be very challenging to train; they often need extra attention, and professional assistance is sometimes necessary.

Puppy instinctively knows that it is being dominated

Understanding fear

Oversee all the puppy's activities to ensure that frightening situations are kept to a minimum. Fears learned at an early age can become lifelong phobias unless they are rapidly overcome.

Rewards and Discipline

Dogs need constant encouragement when they are being trained. Food snacks, toys, and physical contact and verbal praise from their owners are all strong rewards.

Physical punishment should not be used to discipline a dog. Instead, immediately after your dog misbehaves, isolate it for a few minutes, or give it an unpleasant surprise.

TYPES OF REWARDS

Tasty treats
Hold a food treat above the dog's nose to attract its attention. This works best when the dog is hungry.

Reward is held in palm of hand

Even strokes are given with a flat palm

Contact comfort
Physical rewards are important during training, so praise the dog by giving it long strokes along its body.

Rewarding toys
As an incentive, show the dog its favorite toy. You will soon discover which toys it likes best.

Eye contact is made by holding toy above dog's head

SUITABLE REWARDS, AND A BAG TO CARRY THEM IN

CHICKEN-FLAVORED SNACKS

BEEF BONES

BEEF CHUNKS

MIXED-FLAVOR SNACKS

CHEESE-FLAVORED BISCUITS

LIVER AND GARLIC TREATS

GROUND RAWHIDE CHEW STICKS

THROW BALL

CHEW TOY

DRIED FOOD

SQUEAKY BALL

EASY-GRIP TOY

PLASTIC RING

RUBBER BONE

SQUEAKY TOY

WAIST BAG

Every dog has its own personal preferences for snack foods and toys. Observe the dog's behavior and learn what it likes best, then only give these special treats as rewards for good behavior. Food rewards work for most dogs, but some individuals may prefer toys. During training sessions, it is best to keep snacks and small toys in a waist bag or pocket for convenience.

TYPES OF DISCIPLINE

Lonely miscreant
If the dog misbehaves, isolate it from household activity. This is suitable discipline, since most dogs enjoy human companionship. Isolation should only last for a few minutes, and should be followed by release and quiet time.

Common Mistakes

IMPROPER REWARDS
Patting a dog on the head is a dominant gesture, and should never be used as a reward. Instead, stroke the dog along the side of its body.

TOO MANY TOYS
Allow at any one time a maximum of three toys that are unlike any household items. Toys can be rotated to keep them interesting.

UNEXPECTED REWARDS
This dog is scavenging in a garbage can. Avoid situations where the dog receives unplanned rewards like this.

"LEAVE IT"

Isolated dog howls at closed door

Owner uses water pistol to reinforce spoken command

Harsh words
A verbal command, together with an unexpected and unpleasant – but harmless – squirt from a water pistol, may be effective in correcting the misbehavior of some dogs.

Dog reaches out to take food, not expecting discipline

Perfect Timing

When you begin training, make sure your dog knows that rewards are at hand. Praise and reward your dog the instant it responds to your commands. Once your dog has learned your word and hand signals, begin to give fewer food rewards. Reprimand your dog only if you catch it misbehaving. Otherwise it will not know why you are angry.

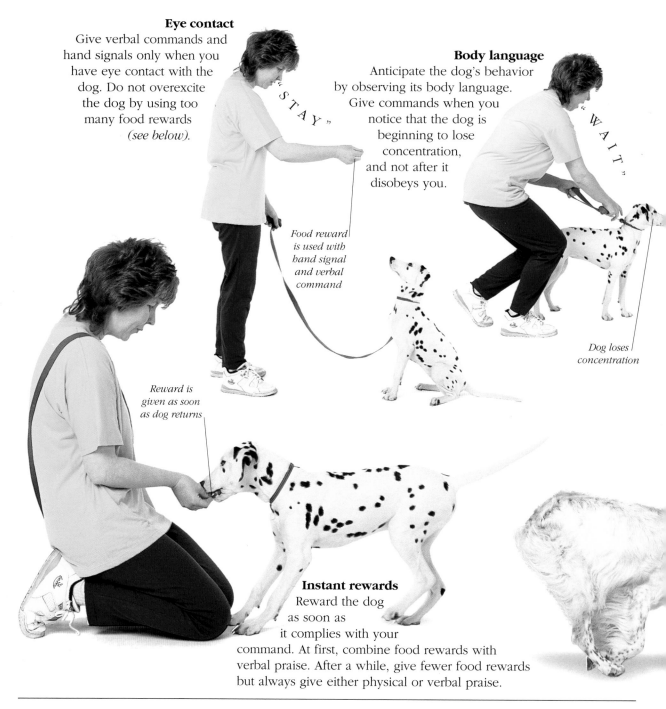

Eye contact
Give verbal commands and hand signals only when you have eye contact with the dog. Do not overexcite the dog by using too many food rewards *(see below)*.

"STAY"

Body language
Anticipate the dog's behavior by observing its body language. Give commands when you notice that the dog is beginning to lose concentration, and not after it disobeys you.

"WAIT"

Food reward is used with hand signal and verbal command

Dog loses concentration

Reward is given as soon as dog returns

Instant rewards
Reward the dog as soon as it complies with your command. At first, combine food rewards with verbal praise. After a while, give fewer food rewards but always give either physical or verbal praise.

Anticipating behavior

Try to anticipate and avoid problem situations. Command the dog's attention before it makes eye contact with another dog, and begins to growl or pull on the lead.

Owner is ready to turn dog's head away

Common Mistakes

SEVERAL DOGS

Training several dogs at once should only be attempted by professional dog trainers. You should train only one dog at a time, while keeping the other dogs out of sight.

INAPPROPRIATE DISCIPLINE

Dog does not understand why its owner is angry

Reprimand the dog only when you actually observe it misbehaving. Displaying anger after the event will simply confuse the dog.

Begging is unacceptable behavior and should not be reinforced

REINFORCEMENT

Rewarding the dog intermittently is the most effective way of reinforcing behavior, but you should only reinforce good behavior.

Unplanned reward

If a dog is protecting its territory, it receives an instant, satisfying, and well-timed reward if the cyclist rides away when chased.

Dog pants with excitement of chase

Giving Commands

Dogs respond best to short, clear commands, given with obvious hand signals. Avoid constantly repeating a command, since this will confuse your dog. Attract your pet's attention by speaking its name, then give your command. The inflection in your voice is important, as are facial expressions. Smile when you are pleased, and scowl at the dog when you are not.

"ROVER"

"ROVER, COME"

Arms held wide to welcome recalled dog

Attracting attention
Use the dog's name to attract its attention. Stand upright, with your shoulders back, and keep the dog's concentration focused on you. Show the dog the food reward as an incentive.

Holding treat in clenched fist prevents dog from snapping

Welcoming body language
Encourage the dog to respond to you by assuming a welcoming posture. Smile, use a friendly and exciting tone of voice, and open your arms to receive the dog.

"NO"

Command is given as dog begins to raise its paws

Firm words
When disciplining the dog, lower your voice and say "No" sharply and deeply. Some people may need to practice using a lower tone of voice.

Stern body language

When the dog misbehaves, assume a commanding posture, and look angry when using negative commands like "No." You should seek professional advice if you have a dog that misbehaves and disobeys you persistently.

Owner's stance is threatening to dog

"SIT"

Dog learns that owner's right arm raised at elbow means "Sit"

Dog watches and listens

Hand signals

Teach the dog to respond to a combination of spoken and visual commands. When the dog is some distance away from you, you can control it by calling its name, then using dramatic hand signals.

Additional Information

UNDERSTANDING LANGUAGE

Dogs have a limited ability to understand the human language. They respond best to short, clear words. To avoid confusion, choose a one- or two-syllable name for the dog, making sure that it is unlike other common words. Do not constantly repeat commands, since this is confusing to dogs. Choose a simple word like "Free" or "Okay" as the release from a command.

THE VALUE OF "NO"

"No" is one of the most important words a dog will learn, since it can prevent it from doing something dangerous. The timing of your commands, and knowing when to say "No," are important elements of dog training. If a shy dog backs away from a stranger, and you try to reassure it by saying "It's okay," you are actually telling it that you approve of its behavior. Instead, say "No" firmly.

BODY LANGUAGE

Dogs are adept at reading human body language. The dog will notice when you are losing concentration or becoming bored with the training session. Be generous with your praise, and dramatic when you reprimand the dog. Always try to maintain the dog's attention by being alert during training.

Putting It All Together

Training should be enjoyable for both you and your dog. Begin training in a quiet environment and increase the distractions over several weeks, until the dog behaves well in any environment. Keep the sessions short, only train when you and your dog are alert, and never issue commands you cannot enforce. End each session on a positive note.

Dog is too tired to train

Short lessons
Dogs have shorter attention spans than humans. You should train the dog for a maximum of 15 minutes, twice a day. Do not attempt to train if either you or the dog are not concentrating.

Primary rewards
Although snacks are good rewards, you should avoid using ones that prevent the dog from concentrating on training. Some dogs respond better to toys, but do not use these if the dog now wants to play instead of continuing with training.

"SIT"

Food is an effective reward for a hungry dog

Optimum time
It is best to train when the dog is hungry. It will be mentally alert, and will respond best to food rewards. Giving a dog two meals a day creates time for two good training sessions.

Reward obedience with dry tidbits

"SIT"

Less potent rewards
Over a few days, reduce the frequency of edible and physical rewards, but always give verbal praise. The dog will soon learn to respond to verbal praise alone.

Dog sits to verbal command alone

Training outdoors

Once the dog reliably obeys commands in the quiet environment of your home, move to a quiet location outdoors and repeat the training sessions. Make sure you are always in a position of control, so that you are able to enforce your commands.

"SIT"

Dog is on lead and under owner's control

Busy environments

Once the dog is obedient both indoors and in quiet outdoor locations, graduate to a busier area.

"SIT"

Dog responds to command in presence of another dog

Enforcing commands

Only give commands if you know you are in control. This dog has been distracted, but because it is on a lead the owner knows she can enforce compliance if the food lure and verbal command are disregarded.

"COME, LIBERTY"

During indoor and outdoor training, dog wears long training lead

Finish with fun

Always finish training with something the dog enjoys and is able to do. Play with the dog, but do not save the greatest rewards for the end of the training session. If you do, the dog will want to end the exercise quickly in order to receive its final reward.

Training is not exercise

Dogs need exercise and time to play with other dogs. Training is not a substitute for either of these, so ensure that the dog gets the exercise its age, breed, and temperament require.

CHAPTER TWO

Early Training

Dogs learn best when they are young and willing and have not learned any bad habits. Do not wait until your puppy is six months old before teaching it basic commands; you should begin training the day your new companion arrives in your home. Provide your puppy with a well-fitting collar, its own private place to sleep and play in quietly, and suitable toys. Base your initial training program around the puppy's feeding schedule by teaching simple commands and rewarding it with its food allowance. Within days, most puppies will come to you and sit on command every time their food is prepared. Make sure your puppy meets other people and animals – under controlled circumstances – while it is young. At an early stage you should introduce it to what will be the routines of its later life.

Early Home Routines

It is best to start training as soon as you bring a new puppy into your home. Teach the puppy your rules before it starts to make its own. All family members should routinely handle a new puppy while it learns to wear a collar and lead, eat only from its own food bowl, sleep in its own bed, come when called, and wait on command. However, only one member of the family should be responsible for actually training the puppy.

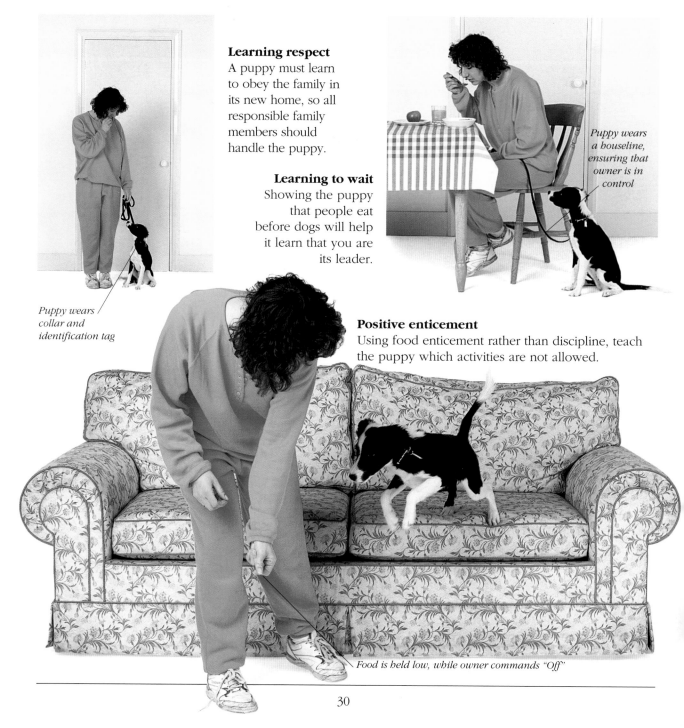

Learning respect
A puppy must learn to obey the family in its new home, so all responsible family members should handle the puppy.

Puppy wears collar and identification tag

Learning to wait
Showing the puppy that people eat before dogs will help it learn that you are its leader.

Puppy wears a houseline, ensuring that owner is in control

Positive enticement
Using food enticement rather than discipline, teach the puppy which activities are not allowed.

Food is held low, while owner commands "Off"

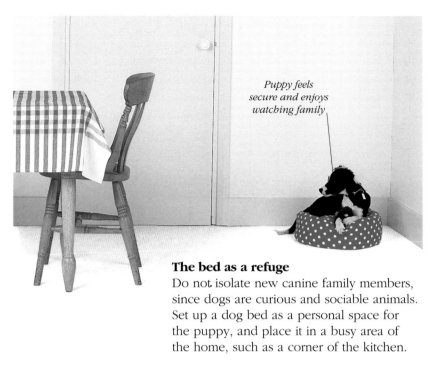

Puppy feels secure and enjoys watching family

Puppy Biting

CURIOUS CHEWING
Puppies investigate their environment by tasting. They play by biting, but you should discipline the puppy when it nips by saying "No" firmly.

BITTER SPRAY
This nontoxic, bitter-tasting spray is available from most pet supply stores.

Apply spray to objects that you do not want dog to chew

The bed as a refuge
Do not isolate new canine family members, since dogs are curious and sociable animals. Set up a dog bed as a personal space for the puppy, and place it in a busy area of the home, such as a corner of the kitchen.

People go first
Dogs naturally want to rush through doors first. By teaching a puppy to wait and allow you to go first, you are demonstrating your leadership. If the puppy does not understand this relationship, training can be difficult.

A private place
Train the puppy to enjoy being left in a crate with its toys *(see page 34)*, leaving it alone for short periods at first. The crate can be moved to your bedroom at night.

"WAIT"

Puppy on lead waits while owner goes through door

Basic Equipment

Choose accessories that are appropriate for the size and temperament of your dog, and replace collars frequently as your puppy grows. You will need a short lead, a long training lead, and an equally long, light houseline to use at home. Body harnesses, head halters, and muzzles are useful for certain types of dogs *(see pages 54–55).*

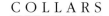

COLLARS

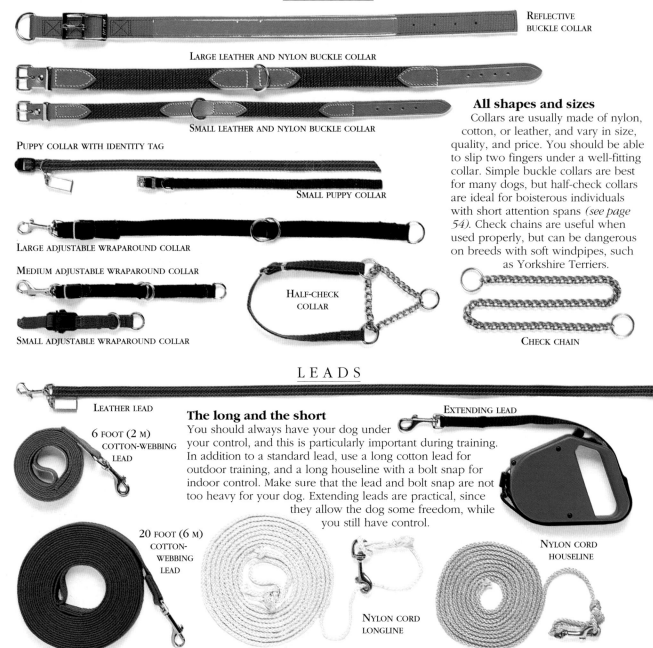

REFLECTIVE BUCKLE COLLAR

LARGE LEATHER AND NYLON BUCKLE COLLAR

SMALL LEATHER AND NYLON BUCKLE COLLAR

PUPPY COLLAR WITH IDENTITY TAG

SMALL PUPPY COLLAR

LARGE ADJUSTABLE WRAPAROUND COLLAR

MEDIUM ADJUSTABLE WRAPAROUND COLLAR

SMALL ADJUSTABLE WRAPAROUND COLLAR

HALF-CHECK COLLAR

CHECK CHAIN

All shapes and sizes

Collars are usually made of nylon, cotton, or leather, and vary in size, quality, and price. You should be able to slip two fingers under a well-fitting collar. Simple buckle collars are best for many dogs, but half-check collars are ideal for boisterous individuals with short attention spans *(see page 54).* Check chains are useful when used properly, but can be dangerous on breeds with soft windpipes, such as Yorkshire Terriers.

LEADS

LEATHER LEAD

6 FOOT (2 M) COTTON-WEBBING LEAD

EXTENDING LEAD

The long and the short

You should always have your dog under your control, and this is particularly important during training. In addition to a standard lead, use a long cotton lead for outdoor training, and a long houseline with a bolt snap for indoor control. Make sure that the lead and bolt snap are not too heavy for your dog. Extending leads are practical, since they allow the dog some freedom, while you still have control.

20 FOOT (6 M) COTTON-WEBBING LEAD

NYLON CORD HOUSELINE

NYLON CORD LONGLINE

HEAD HALTERS AND HARNESSES

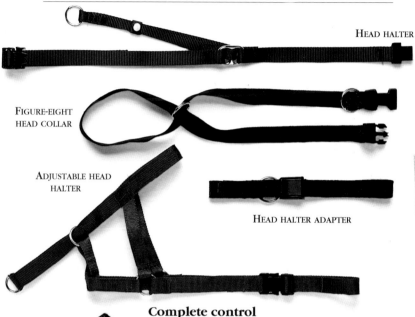

HEAD HALTER

FIGURE-EIGHT
HEAD COLLAR

ADJUSTABLE HEAD
HALTER

HEAD HALTER ADAPTER

Complete control

Head halters *(see page 55)* are ideal for fearful, bold, and independent dogs, as well as for those that mouth and chew excessively. The lead clips to a ring under the dog's jaw. If the dog pulls forward, its own momentum pulls its jaws shut and its head down. Use a body harness on dogs with small heads or soft windpipes *(see page 54)*.

BODY HARNESS

MUZZLES

Bite prevention

Muzzles might appear unpleasant to you, but dogs quickly learn to wear them. Besides their obvious use on potentially aggressive dogs, they are ideal for keeping some destructive dogs from chewing, and for stopping dogs that are prone to scavenging from eating unsavory items. Basket muzzles permit panting and even barking, but a muzzle should not be left on your dog if no one is there to supervise it.

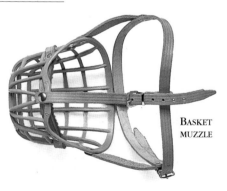

BASKET
MUZZLE

Additional Equipment

BEANBAG BED

PUPPY PLAYPEN

CRATE

HAVENS FOR DOGS

There are many excellent beds made for dogs, while newspaper-lined playpens allow playful activity and controlled house training. Crates are used to keep the dog safe when you are gone.

LIFEJACKET

Dogs swim naturally, but are at risk from drowning if they become exhausted. Dogs should wear lifejackets when they are on boats.

BACKPACK

Physically fit dogs that accompany their owners on hiking or camping trips can carry their own food and bowls in special backpacks.

Crate Training

It might look like a jail to you, but to the dog that has been trained from puppyhood to use it, a crate becomes a favorite place, the dog's own secure haven. Crates should be pleasant places and should never be used for discipline. Crate training encourages house training, reduces potentially destructive behavior, and eases traveling with your dog.

1 Before starting crate training, place soft bedding, a food treat, and an interesting toy inside the crate. Leave the door open initially.

Food treats should be provided in a nontip bowl

2 Using a tasty snack, and the verbal command "Go to your crate," entice the puppy into its new home. Leave the door open so that the puppy can leave the crate at any time.

Puppy willingly enters its personal "den"

3 Once the puppy has become accustomed to the crate, it will continue to use it without any prompting from you.

4 While the puppy plays contentedly, close the crate door for a few minutes. Keep the crate in a busy place like the kitchen.

Puppy plays vigorously with toy

Added Benefits

Puppy is relaxed and feels secure

Crate offers safety in case of an accident

PERSONAL TRANSPORTATION
Problems with traveling are eased if you have a crate-trained puppy. When confined to its own crate, this puppy feels secure in the car.

PEN-FRIENDS
If the playpen is lined with newspaper, puppies can meet and play without causing havoc in your home.

5 The relaxed puppy falls asleep in the security of its crate. Fully crate-trained puppies should not be left in crates for more than two hours during the day, and should be exercised before confinement.

PUPPY PLAYPEN

Having become accustomed to its crate, this puppy is content to be confined to a playpen. Some dogs, especially adopted ones, have a more difficult time with crate confinement, but this rarely happens with puppies.

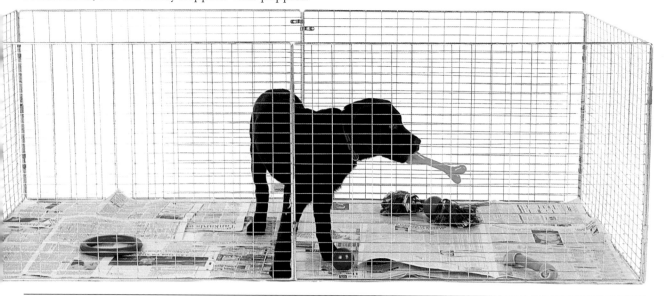

House Training

Some dogs can be house trained quickly, while others take much longer. If you have an adult dog that has never been house trained, treat it as you would a new puppy. Never punish your dog for making a mess in your home. Reprimanding your pet after it has had an accident only teaches it to be nervous and wary of you. Instead, anticipate when your dog needs to eliminate. After your dog wakes up, eats, or plays, take it to the place that you have chosen for it to relieve itself, and always clean up after it. Avoid accidents in the home by restricting your dog to its crate *(see page 34)*, until you have taken it out to eliminate. As your dog relieves itself, use words like "Hurry up," then praise it. Soon your dog will eliminate when you give the "Hurry up" command.

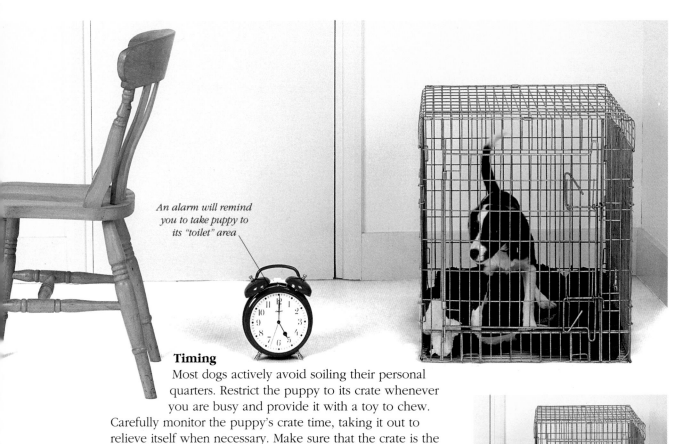

An alarm will remind you to take puppy to its "toilet" area

Timing
Most dogs actively avoid soiling their personal quarters. Restrict the puppy to its crate whenever you are busy and provide it with a toy to chew. Carefully monitor the puppy's crate time, taking it out to relieve itself when necessary. Make sure that the crate is the correct size for the puppy; if it is too big the puppy may soil it.

Paper training
Training the puppy to use newspaper indoors can be confusing to it, since it learns that eliminating indoors is acceptable. Whenever possible, train the puppy to eliminate in an outdoor area, but when circumstances dictate that you use paper indoors, follow the same crate restrictions and let the puppy out onto its newspaper.

Anticipation

A dog that suddenly puts its nose down and sniffs intently is usually signaling that it is about to eliminate. Commercial spray products available from pet stores may or may not induce the puppy to use a designated area.

Puppy sniffs just before urinating

Food, touch, and verbal rewards are given

Instant praise

When taking the puppy outside, keep its attention on you by talking to it or showing it toys, to ensure that there are no accidents on the way. Say "Hurry up" as the puppy eliminates, then praise it for its good behavior.

Create routines

A puppy will need to eliminate after sleeping and playing, and especially after eating or being restricted to its crate. As a general rule, remember that a three-month-old puppy needs to eliminate every three hours.

Owner Training

POINTLESS PUNISHMENT

Control your temper while house training a puppy. Scolding the dog is pointless unless you actually see it eliminating indoors. If you do, say "No" sternly, move the puppy to its designated spot, and praise it.

Dog cowers as owner scolds it

Prevent accidents from occurring by constantly supervising the puppy. If direct supervision is not possible, it is best to keep the puppy in its crate.

RESPONSIBLE BEHAVIOR

Dog feces are not only a public health hazard to both humans and other dogs, but also an aesthetic hazard to the environment. Ensure good relations with the community by always cleaning up after the dog. When you take the dog to a public place, remember to carry a pooper scooper like the one below, or a plastic bag.

Bag is pulled over handle

Use biodegradable bags when possible

Daily Grooming

Grooming your dog daily not only keeps it clean and healthy, but also reasserts your authority over it. Picking up the dog, holding its head, and opening its mouth are dominant gestures, and help reinforce your leadership. Initially, use food rewards as distractions throughout the grooming sessions, then progress to verbal and physical praise alone.

GROOMING EQUIPMENT

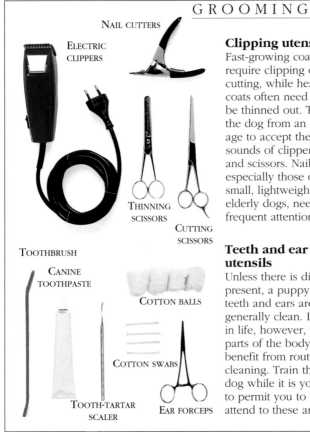

NAIL CUTTERS

ELECTRIC CLIPPERS

THINNING SCISSORS

CUTTING SCISSORS

TOOTHBRUSH

CANINE TOOTHPASTE

COTTON BALLS

COTTON SWABS

TOOTH-TARTAR SCALER

EAR FORCEPS

SLICKER BRUSH

RUBBER BRUSH

FLEA COMB

PIN BRUSH

SOFT PIN BRUSH

SYNTHETIC BRISTLE BRUSH

CHAMOIS CLOTH

WIDE-TOOTHED COMB

STRIPPING COMB

NARROW-TOOTHED COMB

Clipping utensils
Fast-growing coats require clipping or cutting, while heavy coats often need to be thinned out. Train the dog from an early age to accept the sounds of clippers and scissors. Nails, especially those of small, lightweight, or elderly dogs, need frequent attention.

Teeth and ear utensils
Unless there is disease present, a puppy's teeth and ears are generally clean. Later in life, however, these parts of the body benefit from routine cleaning. Train the dog while it is young to permit you to attend to these areas.

Brushes and combs
Brushing the dog daily keeps its coat in top condition. It also reminds the dog that you are the leader. Always use equipment appropriate for the dog's coat type.

GROOMING PREPARATIONS

Dog is on lead for assured control

Picking up a dog
Pick up the dog by putting one arm around its chest and forelimbs, and the other around its rump. Place it on a table for grooming.

Holding a dog still
Hold the dog in the stand position and put your thumb through its collar.

Hand is placed, palm down, under dog's body

Rubber mat is a useful, nonslip surface

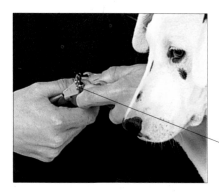

Trimming the nails

It is easiest to cut the nails after the dog has been bathed, when its nails will be softer than usual. Take care not to cut the living tissue (the pink area inside the nail). If in doubt, seek veterinary advice.

Clippers cut white tip of nail

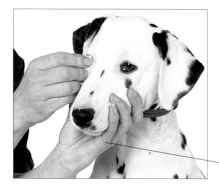

Cleaning the eyes

Many dogs build up mucus in the corners of their eyes. Holding the head firmly, bathe the eyes, using a clean, damp cotton ball for each one. Eye cleaning is best carried out when the dog understands the "Sit" and "Stay" commands *(see page 56)*.

Holding head firmly is a dominant gesture

Examining the mouth

Use food rewards while training the dog to let you open and examine its mouth. You should check the dog's teeth and gums once a week.

Jaw is held gently but firmly

Gentle brushing

Use long, firm strokes to brush along the dog's body. Brush the entire coat, including the tail and legs.

Turning a dog around

Place the flat of your hand, with the fingers together, over the hind-leg muscles to turn the dog around.

Flat palm avoids hurting dog

Special Conditions

LONG COATS

Owner uses slicker brush

Longhaired dogs with thick coats can develop mats on the legs, belly, and behind the ears. Take care when grooming these areas, since the skin here is often quite sensitive.

LIPS AND GUMS

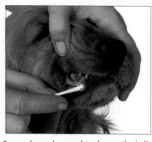

Some breeds need to have their lip folds cleaned, and their gums checked regularly. Use damp cotton swabs to remove any dirt.

HAIRY EARS

Use a damp cotton swab to clean the ears. Have a professional show you how to remove excess hair.

FOOT MAINTENANCE

Minimize the risk of dirt embedding between the toes, by clipping and examining after exercise.

Coming to You

Begin this exercise when your puppy is alert and hungry. Divide your pet's meal into ten equal portions, and throughout the day entice it to the food bowl by using its name and the command "Come." You should never recall the puppy to discipline it, since it will associate returning to you with the unpleasant experience of being reprimanded.

INDOOR TRAINING

"POLLY, COME"

1 Stand a short distance away from the puppy, in a quiet room with no distractions. A hallway is an ideal location. With food visible in your hand, speak the puppy's name, and as it begins to move forward give the command "Come."

Puppy makes eye contact with owner

Food held out to entice puppy

"GOOD DOG"

3 As the puppy approaches, kneel down to get closer to its level. Praise the puppy again and give the food reward while stroking and touching the collar.

2 As the puppy comes to you, praise it by saying "Good dog" in an enthusiastic voice. Encourage the puppy to come to you by bending your knees and opening your arms.

Treat is given immediately puppy returns

Bent knees bring treat closer to puppy

OUTDOOR TRAINING

"POLLY, COME"

Puppy can feel pressure on lead

Puppy is distracted by other dogs

"GOOD DOG"

1 When the puppy is fully trained to come to you indoors, move to a more distracting location. Keep the puppy on a longline or extending lead to ensure compliance, and practice the exercise.

2 Do not use the lead to reel in the puppy; encourage the puppy to return for its reward. A quick jerk on the lead can attract the puppy's attention if it is losing concentration. From a distance, a toy reward is more visible to the puppy than a food reward.

Problem Solving

THE SLEEPY DOG

Dogs – and puppies in particular – have short attention spans, and training is mentally exhausting for them. Train for only five to fifteen minutes at a time, and never train when the dog is tired. Some dogs may require a short period of exercise so that they are physically and mentally prepared for the session. Vary the places in which you train the dog, so that you maintain its interest.

THE UNRESPONSIVE DOG

If the dog does not respond to a food reward, alter its feeding routine, giving fewer meals (but larger quantities). If it still does not respond well to food treats, try using a favorite squeaky toy as a reward.

Squeaky toy attracts puppy's attention

THE DISTRACTED DOG

If the puppy is strong-willed, always carry out any training exercise with it on a lead. This ensures that you can always attract the puppy's attention, and reminds it that it must listen and respond. It will also keep the puppy safe.

"COME"

Sit and Lie Down

Once your puppy responds well to the command to come *(see page 40)*, you can teach it to sit and to lie down. You should practice this exercise with the puppy on the lead, to ensure that you are in control. On completing this routine successfully, your puppy will be able to carry out a sequence of commands for the first time.

THE "SIT" COMMAND

1 Facing the puppy, move away with the lead in your left hand and a food treat in your right. As you command the puppy to come to you, show it the food. It is important to be calm, and not to excite the puppy during this exercise.

Food is held in front of middle of body

"SIT" "GOOD DOG"

2 When the puppy reaches you, slowly move your right hand up and over its head. The puppy will naturally sit down in order to keep its eyes on the food. Give the command "Sit" when you see the puppy begin to bend its hind legs.

Puppy tucks hindquarters into sitting position

Food is held directly above puppy's head

3 Reinforce the sit command from the front and then to the side of the puppy. At first, reward each response with verbal praise and food treats. Gradually reduce the food rewards – eventually words alone will be sufficient.

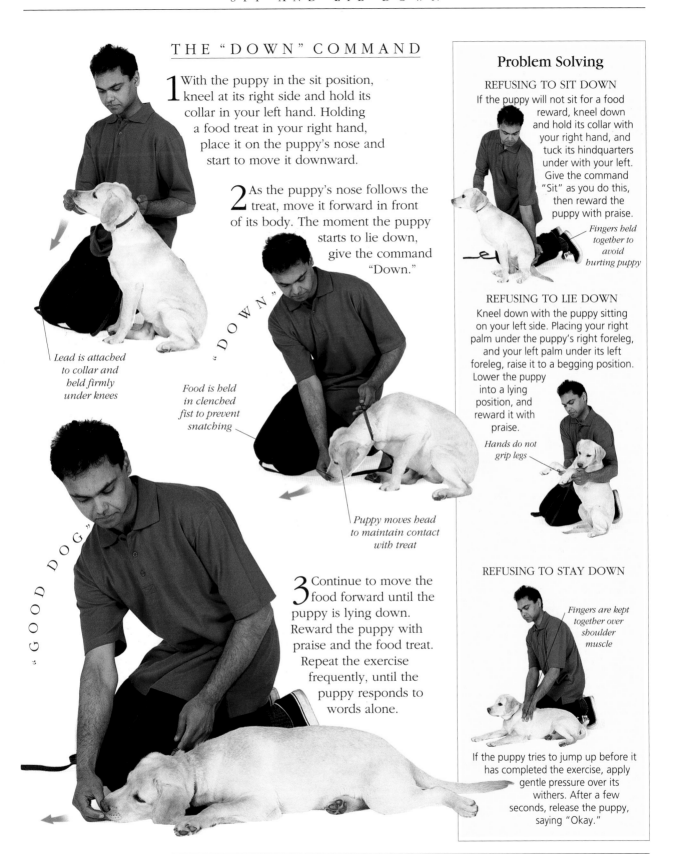

THE "DOWN" COMMAND

1 With the puppy in the sit position, kneel at its right side and hold its collar in your left hand. Holding a food treat in your right hand, place it on the puppy's nose and start to move it downward.

2 As the puppy's nose follows the treat, move it forward in front of its body. The moment the puppy starts to lie down, give the command "Down."

"DOWN"

Lead is attached to collar and held firmly under knees

Food is held in clenched fist to prevent snatching

Puppy moves head to maintain contact with treat

"GOOD DOG"

3 Continue to move the food forward until the puppy is lying down. Reward the puppy with praise and the food treat. Repeat the exercise frequently, until the puppy responds to words alone.

Problem Solving

REFUSING TO SIT DOWN

If the puppy will not sit for a food reward, kneel down and hold its collar with your right hand, and tuck its hindquarters under with your left. Give the command "Sit" as you do this, then reward the puppy with praise.

Fingers held together to avoid hurting puppy

REFUSING TO LIE DOWN

Kneel down with the puppy sitting on your left side. Placing your right palm under the puppy's right foreleg, and your left palm under its left foreleg, raise it to a begging position. Lower the puppy into a lying position, and reward it with praise.

Hands do not grip legs

REFUSING TO STAY DOWN

Fingers are kept together over shoulder muscle

If the puppy tries to jump up before it has completed the exercise, apply gentle pressure over its withers. After a few seconds, release the puppy, saying "Okay."

Walking without a Lead

Outdoor activities are a delight when your dog walks obediently by your side. It is often easiest to train a puppy to walk to heel off the lead at first, since it will enjoy human companionship and will usually be willing to follow its owner. Most puppies will also follow the scent of food snacks, so it is useful to carry treats throughout training.

1 With the puppy on your left side, hold its collar with your left hand and keep a food treat in your right hand. Attract the puppy's attention by speaking its name.

"PRINCE"

2 Walking in a straight line, with the puppy following the food reward, give the command "Heel." Keep your left hand low, ready to grasp the puppy's collar.

"HEEL"

Scent of food attracts puppy

Arm prevents unwanted movement

Puppy concentrates on potential reward

3 Give the command "Wait," and kneel to the puppy's right side, holding the snack low down to discourage jumping. Your left hand, palm down, underneath the puppy's body prevents it from moving.

4 Bending your knees and holding the food near the puppy's nose, make a right turn, repeating the "Heel" command. The puppy must speed up to walk around you.

Arm draws puppy to the right

"HEEL"

Puppy follows treat intently

"STEADY"

5 To make a left turn, use your left hand to guide the puppy by the collar, and give the command "Steady." Hold the food reward low down and move your right hand to the left. The puppy should follow.

Puppy receives reward

Puppy slows down

Problem Solving

LOSING CONCENTRATION
If the puppy's attention wanders, put your left hand under its collar and bring it back to the correct heel position.

Food scent lures distracted puppy

BOISTEROUS BEHAVIOR
If the puppy does not respond to food lures, draw its attention to a favorite toy. Use a longline to ensure the puppy's compliance.

Puppy notices toy

Owner calls puppy's name

JUMPING UP
To discourage jumping, hold the puppy's collar with your left hand and entice it with the hidden reward held low.

Right hand crosses owner's body

ENJOYABLE TRAINING
If the puppy is not interested in one type of food reward, try another, or switch to a favorite squeaky toy. You should keep training sessions short, no more than a few minutes at a time, and always end them with a period of enjoyable play.

Walking on a Lead

Your puppy's safety and well-being depend on you. A dog should never be allowed to run free, unless it is under your supervision in a protected environment, and away from danger. You should have already trained your puppy to sit and to lie down while wearing a lead *(see page 42)*, and to walk with you without wearing a lead *(see page 44)*. Now you can teach it to walk on the lead without pulling.

1 Start training indoors. Let the puppy look at and smell the lead. Then attach the lead to the puppy's well-fitting, comfortable collar *(see page 32)*.

2 With the puppy on your left side, hold the lead and a food reward in your right hand. Your left hand should also hold the slack lead. Command the puppy to sit.

Left hand is ready to slide down lead to collar

H E E L

Lead is given a quick, light jerk

3 Begin to walk, setting off with your left foot. As the puppy walks beside you, give the command "Heel." If the puppy surges forward, slide your left hand down to its collar and gently pull backward.

"GOOD DOG"

4 When the puppy is in the heel position, give the reward and say "Good dog." Then command the puppy to sit, and repeat "Good dog." Gradually increase the distance you cover as the puppy obeys the sequence of commands.

Puppy maintains concentration

Problem Solving

CLIMBING UP THE LEAD
If the puppy tries to jump up on you or climb the lead, sternly say "No" or "Off." Move away, command the puppy to sit, and go back to the beginning of the exercise. Do not train on outdoor walks at first, since these can be too distracting. Train indoors, then slowly graduate to busier locations.

COLLAPSING
If the puppy refuses to move, gently and patiently entice it with a favorite squeaky toy. Do not pull the puppy or become angry. Encourage the puppy with praise, and allow it to build up its confidence.

PULLING FORWARD
Command the puppy to sit each time it pulls. Neither you nor the puppy should lose concentration, and you should not shout the commands. Use a head halter on boisterous dogs.

"STEADY"

"HEEL"

Puppy is close to owner's leg

Owner holds puppy back by its collar

5 Once the puppy is able to walk to heel and sit obediently as you go from room to room, you can train it to turn right. Guide the puppy around to the right with your left hand, and give the command "Heel."

6 To make a left turn, increase your own speed and hold the food in front of the puppy's nose to slow it down. Keep the puppy close to your left leg, and give the command "Steady" as it slows down.

Suitable Toys

Puppies chew objects in order to learn about their environment, but chewing can be an expensive problem. By encouraging your dog to chew its own specific toys, you will prevent it from damaging other household items. Always choose safe toys, and limit their availability to prevent the dog from becoming possessive about them.

TYPES OF TOY

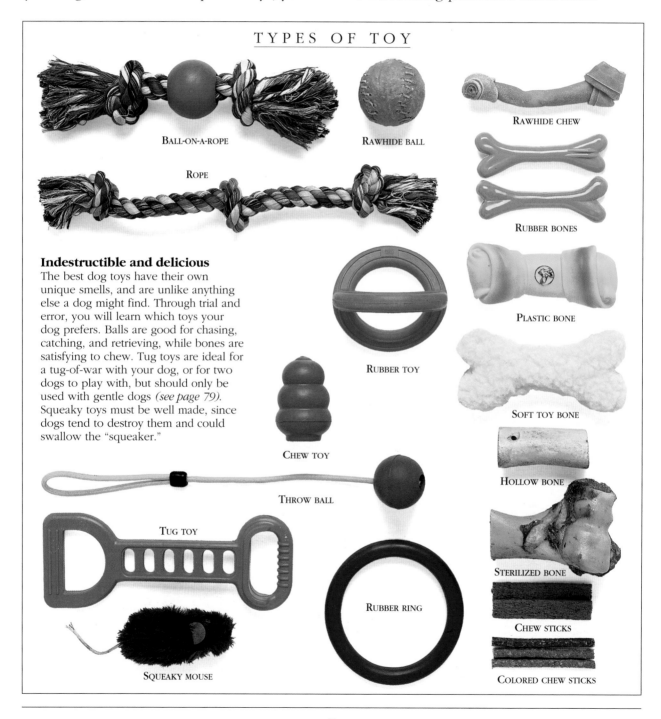

BALL-ON-A-ROPE

RAWHIDE BALL

RAWHIDE CHEW

ROPE

RUBBER BONES

PLASTIC BONE

Indestructible and delicious
The best dog toys have their own unique smells, and are unlike anything else a dog might find. Through trial and error, you will learn which toys your dog prefers. Balls are good for chasing, catching, and retrieving, while bones are satisfying to chew. Tug toys are ideal for a tug-of-war with your dog, or for two dogs to play with, but should only be used with gentle dogs *(see page 79)*. Squeaky toys must be well made, since dogs tend to destroy them and could swallow the "squeaker."

RUBBER TOY

SOFT TOY BONE

CHEW TOY

HOLLOW BONE

THROW BALL

TUG TOY

STERILIZED BONE

RUBBER RING

CHEW STICKS

SQUEAKY MOUSE

COLORED CHEW STICKS

MAKING A CHEW TOY

1 To make a satisfying chew toy for your dog, insert cheese spread into a clean hollow toy or bone.

Cheese spread is inserted deep into hollow

2 Give the object to the dog, who will try to reach the food in the center. You can help the dog reach the last morsel of cheese, deep inside. This is an ideal toy to stimulate a dog when it is at home alone.

Dog enjoys challenge to reach cheese

3 In sight of the dog, put the toy away. Dogs soon learn that toys belong to their owners and are given only on special occasions.

Destructive Chewing

Old shoes smell like new ones

This dog is innocently chewing on its owner's personal items. Avoid giving a dog old clothes or shoes to play with. If dogs are allowed to chew these items, they will assume that they may chew any other articles of clothing. Dogs cannot distinguish between old items and new ones.

TUG-OF-WAR

Soft toy is robust

Dog anchors itself and pulls back

These two dogs are pulling at the same toy. Dogs can be possessive about toys, so if you have two dogs make sure that the toys are not too precious to be fought over.

New Experiences

Enlist the help of friends and neighbors who can provide your puppy with as many varied experiences as possible. If you have your own yard, begin training in it as soon as possible. Unless your vet advises against it, take your puppy to public places so that it becomes accustomed to traffic noise, pedestrians, car trips and, most importantly, to obeying you in a variety of different environments and circumstances. Do not wait for problems to develop. Introduce your puppy to people in uniform, such as letter carriers, to children, and to other adults who look or dress differently from you.

MEETING PEOPLE

Strangers who frighten
A person with a beard, someone wearing a hat, or someone with a complexion unlike that of the dog's human family can be intimidating. Enlisting the help of friends, set up meetings between them and the dog. Reward the dog when it shows curiosity but remains calm.

A positive approach
Instruct children to approach the dog quietly and to stroke it from the side. Reward the dog with verbal praise or a food treat when it behaves calmly.

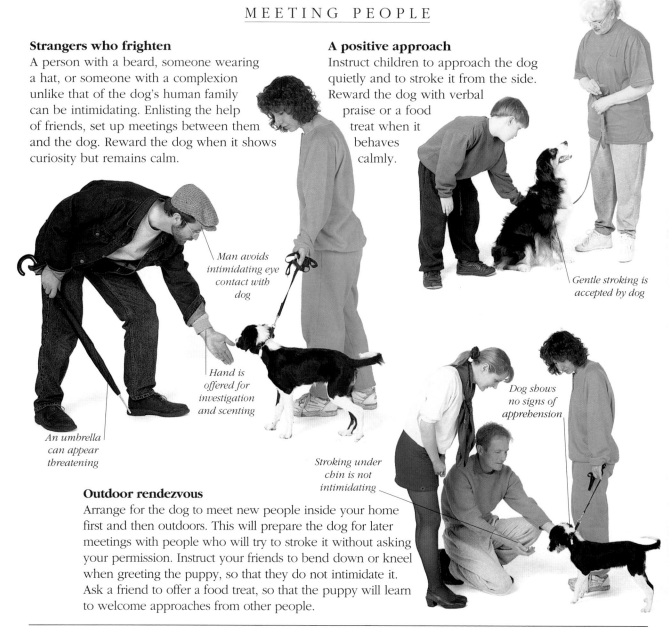

Man avoids intimidating eye contact with dog

Hand is offered for investigation and scenting

An umbrella can appear threatening

Gentle stroking is accepted by dog

Dog shows no signs of apprehension

Stroking under chin is not intimidating

Outdoor rendezvous
Arrange for the dog to meet new people inside your home first and then outdoors. This will prepare the dog for later meetings with people who will try to stroke it without asking your permission. Instruct your friends to bend down or kneel when greeting the puppy, so that they do not intimidate it. Ask a friend to offer a food treat, so that the puppy will learn to welcome approaches from other people.

OUTDOOR TRAINING

Road sense

Once the puppy responds to commands in your home and yard, you can move to busier environments. You should always command the dog to sit before crossing a road.

Hand signals

Hand signals are very important outdoors, where you want the dog to obey even when it is far away from you. You should use dramatic gestures.

Hand is held high so that dog does not miss signal

CAR TRIPS

Lead ensures that owner is in control

Introducing the car

The back of a car can be a frightening place, especially if the dog's first experience in it causes motion sickness and nausea. Before actually driving anywhere, entice the dog into your parked car with a food reward. Once the dog is happy to sit in the car, accustom it to the sound of the engine. Train the dog to look upon the car as a second home *(see page 108)*.

Dog willingly prepares to jump into car, following food reward

Reward quiet behavior

Give food rewards and verbal praise when the dog displays no signs of agitation or nausea. Go for short drives initially and gradually increase their duration. Always reward the dog for settling down and remaining quiet.

Playing with Other Dogs

Although dogs must learn how to behave with humans, they should also be able to play with other dogs. By separating a puppy from its mother and littermates when it is eight weeks old, humans prevent the dog from learning naturally how to behave with its own kind. You can overcome this problem by arranging for the puppy to attend weekly supervised puppy classes *(see page 123)*. The puppy will learn what canine body language means, and how it can use body language when communicating with other dogs. This type of early experience reduces the risks of conflicts later in the dog's life.

Puppy investigates new class member

CHAPTER THREE

Further Training

Once your dog has learned basic commands, you can train it to walk quietly with you, bark only under the correct circumstances, control the use of its paws, hold and retrieve objects, and behave properly with children and other animals. It is important to remember that some dogs are more difficult to train than others. Make training as simple as possible by ensuring that your pet has learned how to behave with other dogs and with people. It is essential that you use collars and leads correctly and choose training equipment suitable for your dog's shape and temperament. Although it is easiest to train a puppy, it is still simple and only slightly more time-consuming to obedience train an adult dog. The result will be a well-mannered and reliable canine companion.

Control and Restraint

It is essential that you use an appropriate form of control when training your dog, and indeed when you are in any public place. Most dogs respond to the pull of a half-check collar, but others are more responsive to head halters or harnesses. Also, where laws or common sense dictate, make sure that your dog wears a muzzle *(see pages 33 and 77)*.

HALF-CHECK COLLAR

1 Make sure you position your dog's half-check collar correctly; the soft webbing should be around its throat, and the chain links should be over the top of its neck.

2 Pull upward on the lead to tighten the collar. This controls unwanted activity in most dogs without causing discomfort. Avoid using check collars on dogs with delicate windpipes.

Hook-on lead is attached to collar ring

Fabric lies comfortably across delicate windpipe

BODY HARNESSES

Emergency harness
Loop the lead across the dog's chest and hold it close to its body. This enables you to retain firm control of the dog if it becomes frightened and pulls unexpectedly.

Lead is threaded through handle

Correcting harness
With the harness correctly positioned, the dog is controlled by tension to the rib cage. A harness is suitable for breeds with soft windpipes, such as Yorkshire Terriers, and for those with muscular necks, such as Pugs.

Harness fits securely around chest

HEAD HALTER

1 Slip the head halter over the dog's muzzle, putting your hand under its jaw to hold its head up.

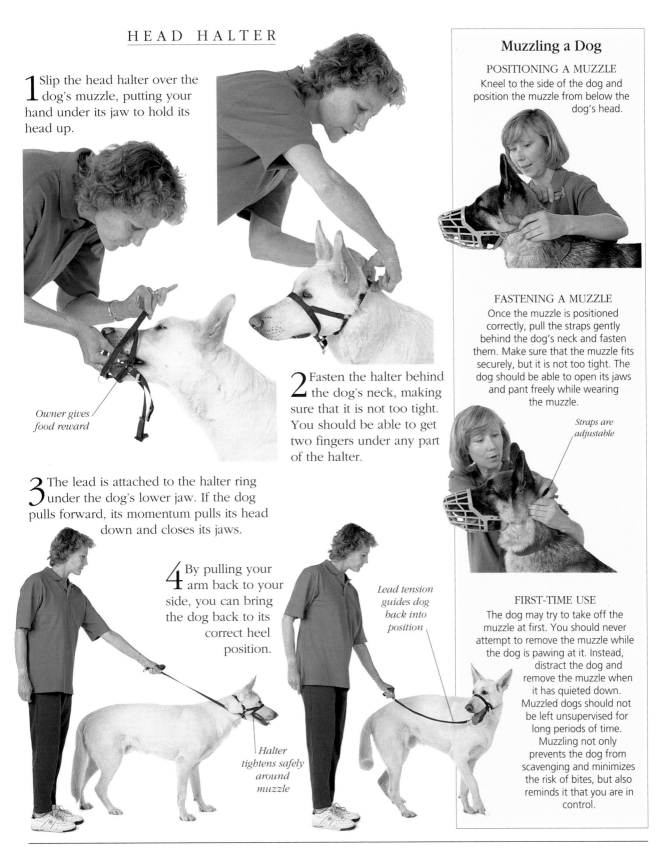

Owner gives food reward

2 Fasten the halter behind the dog's neck, making sure that it is not too tight. You should be able to get two fingers under any part of the halter.

3 The lead is attached to the halter ring under the dog's lower jaw. If the dog pulls forward, its momentum pulls its head down and closes its jaws.

4 By pulling your arm back to your side, you can bring the dog back to its correct heel position.

Halter tightens safely around muzzle

Lead tension guides dog back into position

Muzzling a Dog

POSITIONING A MUZZLE
Kneel to the side of the dog and position the muzzle from below the dog's head.

FASTENING A MUZZLE
Once the muzzle is positioned correctly, pull the straps gently behind the dog's neck and fasten them. Make sure that the muzzle fits securely, but it is not too tight. The dog should be able to open its jaws and pant freely while wearing the muzzle.

Straps are adjustable

FIRST-TIME USE
The dog may try to take off the muzzle at first. You should never attempt to remove the muzzle while the dog is pawing at it. Instead, distract the dog and remove the muzzle when it has quieted down. Muzzled dogs should not be left unsupervised for long periods of time. Muzzling not only prevents the dog from scavenging and minimizes the risk of bites, but also reminds it that you are in control.

Sit and Stay

The commands "Sit" and "Stay" form the basis of responsible pet ownership and are useful forms of control during outdoor activity. Begin training in a quiet indoor area such as a hallway, and limit each session to 15 minutes. Once your dog has learned to respond consistently to your word commands, you may use simple hand signals *(see page 62)*.

1 With the dog on your left side, hold the gathered lead at waist level in your left hand, and a food reward in your right. As the dog sits, in order to concentrate on the treat, give the command "Sit" *(see page 42)*.

"STAY"

2 Maintaining tension on the lead, step forward with your right foot. Give the command "Stay" as you move forward.

Body turns toward dog

Food treat is palmed but obvious

Dog looks up intently

3 Maintaining eye contact with the dog, move your left foot to join your right foot.

4 Exerting light pressure on the lead and holding it over the dog's head, turn to face the dog. Keep its concentration by holding the food reward high above its head.

Feet do not move and there are no signs of jumping up

5 Reward the dog for staying. Now slowly walk around the dog, holding the lead above its head. Issue as few commands as possible, so that you do not confuse the dog. Give quiet praise.

Dog senses contact through taut lead

Dog obediently remains still

6 After several sessions, the dog should sit and stay while on the lead. Now drop the lead and repeat each of the five previous steps, always praising the dog for good behavior.

Owner keeps her hands by her sides

Dog concentrates on owner, waiting for command or reward

7 When the dog obediently sits and stays with the lead dropped, give it the reward. It is important to give rewards while the dog is doing what you command, not after it has moved.

"GOOD DOG"

Food reward is held up to maintain eye contact

"OKAY"

8 After you have rewarded the dog, release it from the training session by opening your arms and saying "Okay."

If the Dog Moves

You are teaching the dog a completely new language, so do not expect it to understand the commands immediately. If the dog moves, or if it does not naturally sit and stay in order to observe its potential food reward, hold it by the collar with your left hand and tuck its bottom down with your right.

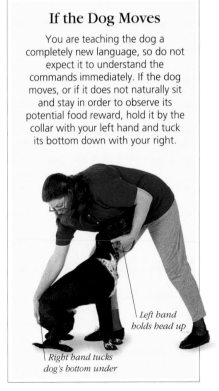

Left hand holds head up

Right hand tucks dog's bottom under

Come and Sit

You will often notice potential dangers before your dog does, so teaching it to return to you on command is essential for its safety. As a puppy your dog comes to you for security, but as an adult it should be trained to return because it wants to be with you. Recall training is rewarding and fun, and the best results are obtained when a reliable bond has been established between you and your canine companion.

"STAY"

1 The dog should have previously learned to sit and stay *(see page 56)*. With the lead in your left hand and a food treat in your right, walk away giving the command "Stay."

Lead is gathered in left hand

Eye contact between dog and owner is maintained

"SIT"

Food is held close to body

2 Turn to face the dog, holding it on the lead, and show it the food reward. Call the dog, using its name and the command "Come."

3 As the dog reaches you, give the command "Sit." Many dogs will naturally sit in order to keep an eye on the reward, but you should still issue the command as the dog sits down.

"PRINCE, COME"

Owner waves toy

4 Once the dog has learned to return to you on a standard lead, progress to a longline. A toy reward may be more visible to the dog from a distance.

Longline is slack but ensures compliance with command

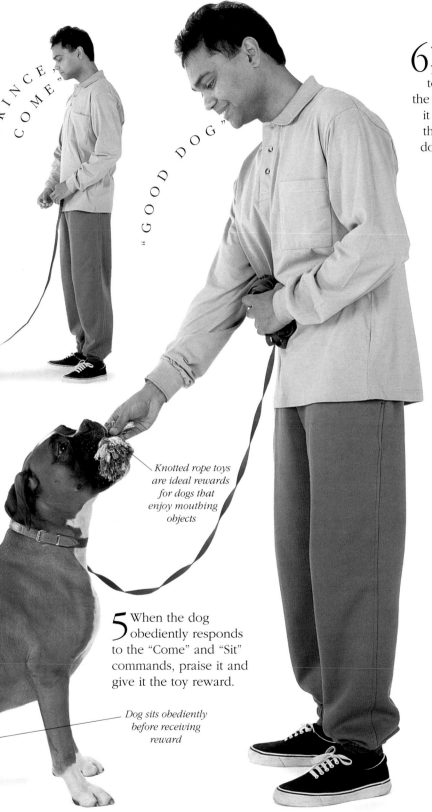

"PRINCE, COME"

"GOOD DOG"

"SIT"

6 With the dog's lead over your shoulder and the toy in your pocket, call the dog and command it to sit. Proceed to this stage once the dog reliably comes to you on the longline.

Reward is visible to dog

Dog sits on hearing command

Knotted rope toys are ideal rewards for dogs that enjoy mouthing objects

5 When the dog obediently responds to the "Come" and "Sit" commands, praise it and give it the toy reward.

Dog sits obediently before receiving reward

Extra Information

HAVE PATIENCE

The "Sit," "Stay," and "Come" commands are the most important lessons you can teach a dog, since they are the basis of a well-mannered dog. All dog owners have a responsibility for ensuring that their pets are not a nuisance. Praise the dog when it responds well and always use a positive tone of voice. When it does not obey a command, repeat the exercise from the previous level of success.

HAVE FUN

Training should be fun for both you and the dog. Use rewards freely at first, and soon the dog will come to you because it enjoys your company. Always finish training sessions with games or play, so that the dog will look forward to the next lesson. Be theatrical during exercises that involve moving around, because dogs enjoy this.

Lie Down

Training your dog to lie down reliably on your command is a valuable lesson, especially during outdoor activity where there are dangers such as busy roads. Your dog will also learn that you are in control, which is particularly important if it is a dominant and assertive individual. There are two lying down positions: "sphinx," in which the hind legs are tucked under, and "flat," where the hips are rolled and the legs are to one side.

Fingers are under collar

Dog concentrates on food reward

Lead is secured under knees

Owner controls movement by holding collar

Hand makes an L-shape

1 With the dog on the lead on your left side, command it to sit *(see page 42).* Kneel down and tuck the lead under your knees. Hold the dog's collar with your left hand, and hold a food reward in your right palm.

2 With the food hidden in your closed fist, let the dog smell the scent. This focuses the dog's mind, while your hand under the collar prevents the dog from moving forward.

3 Move your right hand straight down, then forward between the dog's forepaws. As the dog drops to follow the food, give the command "Down."

4 As soon as the dog lies down, give the food reward. At this stage, it does not matter which position the dog assumes, as long as it is comfortable.

Dog begins to assume relaxed position

EMERGENCY ACTION

To put the dog into the instant down position, bend your knees, slide your hand down the lead to the collar, and pull down, locking your wrist and elbow. Issue the command "Down." Reward the dog with praise when it is in the down position. Training the dog to lie down indoors, or in a quiet garden where there are few distractions, is easier than training in more stimulating surroundings. Once the dog has mastered the lesson in a relatively quiet place, you will be able to move to a more stimulating environment.

Problem Solving

"DOWN"

Owner pulls downward on collar

REINFORCING THE DOWN

If the dog's shoulders rise from the down position before it has been released, run your hand firmly down the lead to the collar. This controls the upward movement, and exerts pressure downward. As the dog goes back down, repeat the command "Down." The dog should only leave the down position when you say "Okay."

RELUCTANT DOGS

If the dog is not food-oriented, try changing the reward. Use a chew toy that the dog is obsessed with *(see page 94)*. Only physically assist dogs into the down position *(see page 43)* if they accept being touched. If you have a dominant dog, only use rewards. If these methods fail, enlist professional help.

AVOIDING INJURY

Do not apply pressure over delicate areas such as the kidney, rib cage, bladder, and liver regions.

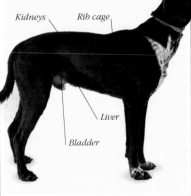

Kidneys *Rib cage*

Liver

Bladder

Owner gives authoritative command

Dog is guided down firmly and quickly

Head goes down first

Down and Stay

Jumping up on people and chasing are part of natural dog behavior, but they can be unpleasant and even dangerous activities. By teaching your dog to stay down on command you can control these unwanted actions. Use verbal commands and rewards, but also use simple hand signals so that your dog can understand your commands from a distance.

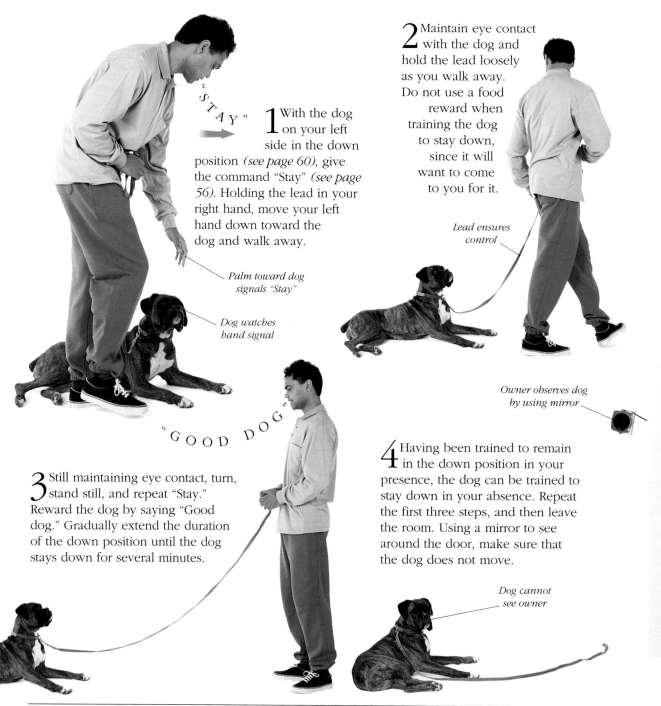

"STAY"

1 With the dog on your left side in the down position *(see page 60)*, give the command "Stay" *(see page 56)*. Holding the lead in your right hand, move your left hand down toward the dog and walk away.

Palm toward dog signals "Stay"

Dog watches hand signal

2 Maintain eye contact with the dog and hold the lead loosely as you walk away. Do not use a food reward when training the dog to stay down, since it will want to come to you for it.

Lead ensures control

Owner observes dog by using mirror

"GOOD DOG"

3 Still maintaining eye contact, turn, stand still, and repeat "Stay." Reward the dog by saying "Good dog." Gradually extend the duration of the down position until the dog stays down for several minutes.

4 Having been trained to remain in the down position in your presence, the dog can be trained to stay down in your absence. Repeat the first three steps, and then leave the room. Using a mirror to see around the door, make sure that the dog does not move.

Dog cannot see owner

5 After a few minutes, return to the dog and give the verbal reward "Good dog." You should reward the dog calmly and quietly when it is still lying down. Do not excite the dog, and do not reward it for getting up.

"GOOD DOG"

6 Release the dog from the down position with the word "Okay." Do not excite the dog by being too flamboyant, because excitement is such a good reward that the dog will only look forward to the end of the exercise, and not to the training itself.

Dog rises up eagerly

Open palm signals release

Problem Solving

DISOBEYING COMMANDS
If the dog moves while you are observing it through the mirror, go back into the room and move around in the dog's sight while it is still in the down position.

DISTRACTING THE DOG
To prepare for training the dog in distracting environments, make loud noises while you are watching it through the mirror. As the dog starts to move, go back into the room and repeat the command "Down." Do not rush toward the dog or display anger, since this will make it excited.

PRACTICAL USES

You should train the dog to remain lying down even when unexpected activity occurs. This not only ensures the safety of the dog and other people, but also displays its obedient behavior.

Dog lies completely relaxed

Long Down

The results of training your dog to lie down on command for an extended period of time will be satisfying for both you and your pet. You will be able to take your dog on shopping trips, or even to your workplace, fully confident that when you tell it to lie down it will be in the same position 20 minutes later. This exercise requires patient training, but it is worth the extra time and effort to have a reliable canine companion.

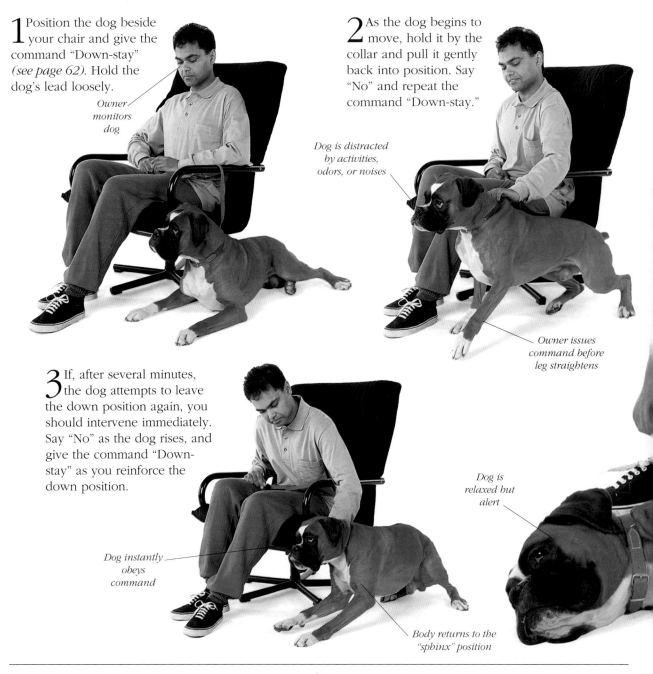

1 Position the dog beside your chair and give the command "Down-stay" *(see page 62)*. Hold the dog's lead loosely.

Owner monitors dog

2 As the dog begins to move, hold it by the collar and pull it gently back into position. Say "No" and repeat the command "Down-stay."

Dog is distracted by activities, odors, or noises

Owner issues command before leg straightens

3 If, after several minutes, the dog attempts to leave the down position again, you should intervene immediately. Say "No" as the dog rises, and give the command "Down-stay" as you reinforce the down position.

Dog instantly obeys command

Dog is relaxed but alert

Body returns to the "sphinx" position

4 After a while, the dog should assume a more comfortable resting position on its side. Whereas it is easy for the dog to instantly leave the "sphinx" position *(see page 60)*, once it lies on its side it has accepted your command for a long down.

Important Lessons

BOSSY DOGS
In training the dog to stay in the down position for an extended period of time, you are telling it that you are the leader and also teaching it to be calm. If you think you have a dominant dog, command it to assume a long down position at least once a day to remind it of your established leadership.

EXTRA VALUES
This exercise is an invaluable way of preventing the dog from frightening children, stealing food, or jumping up on people. This type of training can be frustrating and time-consuming, but you will eventually have a canine companion who is easy to control.

5 Twenty minutes later the dog should still be in a fully relaxed position. Increase the duration of this exercise gradually over several training sessions, until the dog is completely reliable.

Bark Control

A barking dog offers protection and makes an excellent burglar alarm, but you do need an on-off switch. When your dog has learned to "speak" on command you will be able not only to control its barking, but also to command it to be quiet. Once the dog knows that barking is only permitted under specific circumstances, it can be trained to bark on command, or on hearing such sounds as smoke alarms or noises outside a window. You should initially train to rewards like food and toys, using verbal praise, too.

1 Attach the dog's lead to a fence or post, and stand about 3 feet (1 m) away. Tease the dog by showing it a toy, and give a food reward when it barks with frustration.

Food is ready to be given at moment of barking

Alert dog concentrates on activity

2 Put the toy away, and change the reward from a food treat to a verbal "Good dog" when the dog barks, giving a food treat only occasionally.

"GOOD DOG"

Toy is in pocket

3 Give the command "Speak" the moment the dog barks, then give the toy as a reward. Correct timing is essential here, and by observing the dog's body language you can anticipate the bark *(see page 22).*

"SPEAK"

Barking dog is rewarded with toy

4 Once the dog understands the command "Speak", give the command "Quiet" when the dog is barking. Give the toy reward as soon as the dog stops barking, but put the toy away and command "No" if it continues.

"NO"

Owner does not give reward to barking dog

5 After teaching the dog to bark or be quiet when you are near, move a short distance away from it. Patiently repeat the exercise from the beginning, until the dog learns to respond to the commands.

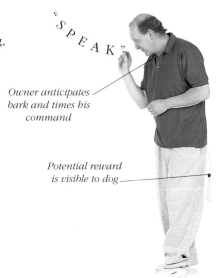

"SPEAK"

Owner anticipates bark and times his command

Potential reward is visible to dog

6 Return to the dog and reward it with its favorite toy. Continue repeating the exercise until the dog consistently responds to intermittent rewards while secured to the fence. Then release the dog from the fence and continue training.

Dog is rewarded by being allowed to chew toy

Dog has not moved

Useful Variations

ALTERNATIVE "QUIET"
If the dog is food-oriented, try putting a tasty morsel of food on its nose to stop it from barking. Timing your command perfectly, say "Quiet" as the dog stops barking, then give the food treat. Only reward the dog when it is silent.

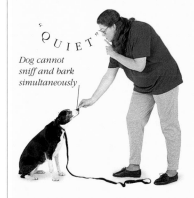

"QUIET"

Dog cannot sniff and bark simultaneously

Owner senses danger

"GUARD"

Dog barks on command

PROTECTION
Most people only require their dog to bark as a means of defense, so teaching the command "Guard" rather than "Speak" is a useful option. A barking dog is a good deterrent against intruders in the home, or against potential attackers outdoors.

Learning to Touch

Training a dog to use its paw teaches it dexterity, and some dogs are more adept at this than others. It is a way in which dogs can communicate, and is also the basis for "shaking hands" – a valuable game, since raising a paw is a subservient gesture. By training your dog to carry out this exercise, you are reinforcing your pack-leader status.

1 With the dog on your left side, command it to sit. Kneeling down, hold the dog's collar in your left hand, and show it the food you have concealed in your right hand.

Dog concentrates on potential treat

2 Move your right hand down to the floor, until it is in front of the dog's paws. Hold the collar to prevent the dog from lying down.

Dog is restrained from putting muzzle near food reward

3 Push the treat toward the dog's paws. As the dog lifts its paw, move your clenched hand under it, and then slightly up off the floor. Continue to restrain the dog by the collar.

Paw makes contact with owner's hand

"PAW"

4 With the dog's paw resting on your fist, lift it up and give the command "Paw." Then give the food reward. Repeat the exercise, using "Paw" to elicit the response, and praising.

5 Once the dog consistently raises its paw to your hand on verbal command alone, show it that you are concealing a food reward behind a small piece of plywood.

Food snack is hidden from view

Excessive Pawing

If the dog demands attention by pawing at you excessively, say "No" firmly and command it to lie down. Be aware, however, that the dog is letting you know that it needs mental and physical stimulation.

Owner uses stern tone of voice

Contact is used to seek attention

Dog exercises reflexes, and catches object in midair

6 Give the command "Paw," and reward the dog with the food treat when it touches the plywood. This is the basis for a variety of touch games.

Touching panel with paw releases toy

TOUCH GAME

Once the dog has learned how to use its paw on command, it can be trained to open doors and play mentally stimulating games. Touching a panel on this box ejects an object for the dog to catch.

Walking to Heel

It is useful if your dog knows how to sit obediently *(see page 56)* before you train it to walk to heel. Start training in a quiet room, walking toward a door that does not lead outdoors. Gradually increase distractions until the dog walks to heel out of the front door without becoming overexcited. If your dog is powerful or boisterous, using a head halter will give you the best control *(see page 55)*. Avoid constantly repeating the "Heel" command.

1 Start training with the dog in the sit position on your left side. Hold the gathered lead and a food reward in your right hand, and hold the other end of the lead close to the dog's collar with your left hand.

2 Using the dog's name and the command "Heel," begin to walk, leading with your left foot. Keep the dog close to your left thigh. Give the food reward when the dog has walked to heel for a few paces.

Lead is held in both hands

"SHEP, HEEL"

"SHEP, HEEL"

Dog follows food reward

Lead is slack

3 When the dog is able to walk 20 paces without restraint, use a food reward as an inducement to turn right.

Light jerks on lead will bring dog back into position

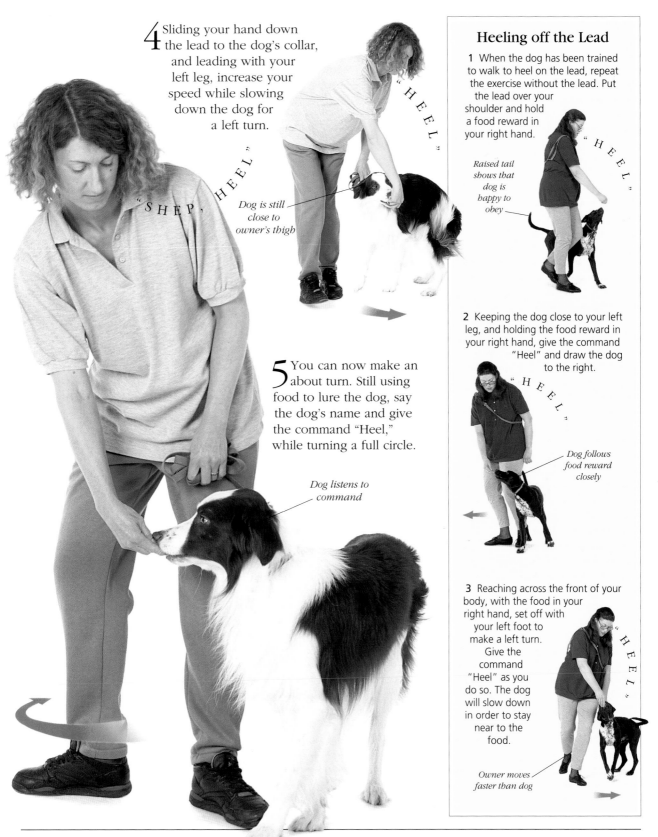

4 Sliding your hand down the lead to the dog's collar, and leading with your left leg, increase your speed while slowing down the dog for a left turn.

"SHEP, HEEL"

"HEEL"

Dog is still close to owner's thigh

5 You can now make an about turn. Still using food to lure the dog, say the dog's name and give the command "Heel," while turning a full circle.

Dog listens to command

Heeling off the Lead

1 When the dog has been trained to walk to heel on the lead, repeat the exercise without the lead. Put the lead over your shoulder and hold a food reward in your right hand.

"HEEL"

Raised tail shows that dog is happy to obey

2 Keeping the dog close to your left leg, and holding the food reward in your right hand, give the command "Heel" and draw the dog to the right.

"HEEL"

Dog follows food reward closely

3 Reaching across the front of your body, with the food in your right hand, set off with your left foot to make a left turn. Give the command "Heel" as you do so. The dog will slow down in order to stay near to the food.

"HEEL"

Owner moves faster than dog

Holding Objects

One of the most enjoyable games that you can play with your dog involves fetching objects *(see page 74)*. However, first the dog must learn to hold an object in its mouth. Do not use squeaky toys in this exercise, since your dog will want to chew them. Use a small piece of rolled-up carpet or a special retrieve dummy. It is best to reward with verbal and physical praise – not food treats – since the dog must continue to hold the object.

HOLDING AN OBJECT

1 Kneel beside the dog, who should be sitting. Hold the lead under your knees and your left arm around the dog's head. Gently open the dog's mouth, saying "Good dog."

Jaw is opened gently with thumb

Fingers feel jaw tension

"HOLD"

2 Having previously teased the dog with the training object, and after you have made sure that it is not unhappy, hold the dog's head up and put the object into its mouth. Now give the command "Hold."

3 The dog should hold the object willingly and correctly just behind its canine teeth, with its tongue retracted. Praise the dog by saying "Good dog to hold."

"GOOD DOG TO HOLD"

Object is gripped comfortably

PICKING UP AN OBJECT

1 Now you can teach the dog to pick up the object. Tease the dog by bringing the object up to its nose.

"GOOD DOG"

Dog concentrates on object

Dog can smell and see object

Owner kneels on lead

2 Move the object down towards the floor. The dog should be interested and should follow the object intently. Give the verbal reward "Good dog."

3 Rest the object on the floor, but do not take your hand away. Command "Hold" as the dog moves forward to take the object in its mouth.

"HOLD"

4 Remove your hand from the object, and the dog should pick it up. At the same moment, repeat the command "Hold," ensuring that the dog does not drop the object.

Problem Solving

"BAH"

Object is reinserted

Dog is held in position

REJECTING THE OBJECT
If the dog attempts to spit out the object, say "Bah!" and hold it in place. Do not say "Hold" at this stage, or the dog will associate that word with an experience of holding that it does not enjoy. Go back to the beginning of the exercise.

AVOIDING THE OBJECT
If the dog turns its head away from the object, follow the dog's head and always keep the object at nose level.

Object is kept close to dog's nose

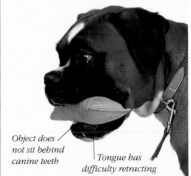

Object does not sit behind canine teeth

Tongue has difficulty retracting

DIFFICULT HOLDS
Some dogs, such as Boxers, have overshot jaws, so they must hold objects in front of, rather than behind, their canine teeth.

Retrieving Objects

Once your dog has learned to hold and pick up an object, it is ready to learn to chase it and bring it back to you. If you are training a puppy, use a squeaky toy initially and let the puppy play with it. Otherwise, use the same object that you used in the previous exercise *(see page 72)*. These exercises offer your dog mental and physical stimulation.

1 With the dog's lead attached for guaranteed control, hold the dog by its collar with one hand as you throw the object a short distance.

Dog watches object

2 Give the command "Fetch" as you release your hold on the dog's collar. Having been trained to pick up and hold the object, the dog should now chase it.

"FETCH"

Dog on lead is under owner's control

3 Once the dog has picked up the object, give the command "Come" to recall it. Crouch down to encourage the dog, and give gentle jerks on the lead if necessary.

"COME"

Dog grips object firmly

4 Reward the dog for its obedience with firm strokes down its side and the verbal praise "Good dog." Put your hand under the dog's jaw to prevent it from dropping the object.

G O O D

D O G

Dog remains standing

5 Issue the command "Give," and take the object from the dog's mouth. As soon as the dog releases the object, reward it with the words "Good dog."

"G I V E"

Dog relinquishes object

6 Reminding the dog that you are still in control, command it to sit. Give the object back to the dog as a final reward.

Problem Solving

RELUCTANT TO FETCH
If the dog is unwilling to fetch the object, make the game more interesting by using a squeaky toy and running with the dog on its lead to where you have thrown the object. Gradually increase the distance that you throw the toy.

RELUCTANT TO HOLD
If the dog runs to the object but then appears to be puzzled, it has not learned to hold properly. Teach the "Hold" command again *(see page 72)*, using a more interesting toy.

RELUCTANT TO RETURN
If the dog picks up the object but does not respond to your command to come, go back to recall training *(see page 58)* before continuing the retrieve exercise.

DROPPING THE OBJECT
A dog that picks up the thrown object, and starts carrying it back but then drops it, needs more lessons in holding *(see page 72)*. When the dog is proficient in this exercise, continue with the retrieve routine, starting with short distances and gradually increasing them.

PUPPY RETRIEVING
You can turn this exercise into a game to play with a puppy. Let the puppy chew the toy, and do not try to take it away. Praise the puppy when it naturally drops the object. Puppies usually take their toys to a "safe place," so you should begin by throwing the object from there.

Arms held wide to attract puppy

Toy feels exciting to carry

Dogs and Children

It is just as important to train children how to approach dogs as it is to train dogs how to behave with children. You should teach your children that not all dogs are friendly, and that they should always ask the owner's permission before touching a dog. Instruct them never to rush up to a dog, or to tease it or shout at it. Children should not be given responsibility for training or feeding a dog until they are mature and sensible.

No eye contact
You should ensure that children make eye contact with you rather than the dog. Because children are smaller and less authoritative than adults, they are more at risk from bites.

Boy looks at owner and asks to stroke dog

Gentle strokes
Instruct children to stroke the dog from the side, not from the front, and tell them that they should never pat the dog's head. Praise the dog for its good behavior, but be prepared to reprimand it whenever it snaps or growls.

Boy gives long strokes along dog's side

Excitement and obedience
Train the dog to lie down, even in the presence of exciting activity such as children playing with a ball. Some dogs nip and chew in a playful context, so do not leave them alone with small children.

Dog is alert but relaxed in presence of children

Canine manners

Teach the dog not to grab food from children by training it to take food only on command *(see page 121)*. Reward the dog for sitting obediently while a child eats.

Adult responsibilities

Children should feed the dog only from its food bowl, under the supervision of an adult.

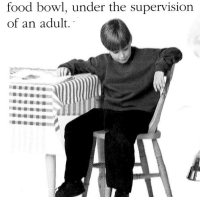

This dog is not frightened by children

Introductions to infants

Allow a new dog to scent and investigate a child only if you are sure the dog is reliable, and only in your presence.

Safety first

A dog should wear a muzzle in the presence of toddlers. This is particularly important if the dog guards or chases. If it has ever threatened or bitten anyone, a professional trainer should be consulted.

Meeting the New Baby

Dog is interested in baby

Baby is present when dog is fed

Allow the dog to see and smell, but not to touch, a new baby. You should praise, play with, and feed the dog in the baby's presence. An infant's squeals and jerky movements can stimulate nervous behavior, and if you are worried you should seek professional help.

Games with Dogs

Dogs thrive on both mental and physical stimulation. They are also inquisitive, and enjoy human companionship. By playing constructive games with your dog, you can alleviate boredom, channel its natural jumping behavior, and reduce any destructive activity. By controlling the games, you will reinforce your leadership.

Frisbee games
Catching a Frisbee and returning it is an exciting game for active, healthy dogs, but can be physically demanding, and even dangerous, for elderly or overweight animals.

Arms are held open to welcome dog

Use special pet toys with rounded edges

Dog jumps to catch ball

Playing with balls
Catch and drop is a simple game that tests the dog's reactions and obedience. Use soft tennis balls, since these are unlikely to harm the dog's teeth, and avoid using potentially damaging hard-rubber balls, or golf balls.

Activity games
Train the dog to participate in sponsored activities and games. Many dog clubs hold competitions involving these, and it is enjoyable for both you and the dog to participate in them.

"Flying mouse" is ejected from box when dog touches lever

Hide-and-seek
Playing hide-and-seek with the dog tests its mental and scenting abilities. Alternatively, train the dog to seek out hidden objects like a set of keys, a wallet, a shoe, or a slipper – but only on your command.

Owner hides behind door

Additional Information

USING TOYS
When you have finished playing with the dog, make a point of putting the toys away, preferably in their own bag or box. The dog will soon learn that the toys belong to you, and that it is only allowed to play with them under your terms. This makes the toys more desirable, so that you can use them as potent rewards during or after training. They are also useful as play objects when the dog is left at home alone.

REWARDING GAMES
Playing games can be rewarding for both you and the dog. If possible, play games after each training session. You should avoid playing before training, since the dog will then be too tired to concentrate properly. You can incorporate training into your games by reinforcing the "Come," "Sit," "Stay," "Down," and "Drop" commands throughout, and by using play as the reward. If family members and friends participate in the games, the dog will receive rewards from a variety of people, and will learn to enjoy the companionship of all humans.

Toy is designed for retrieving, chewing, and tug-of-war

Tug-of-war
Only play tug-of-war when the dog learns to drop an object on command *(see page 75)*, and always use specially made, robust toys. Never play "mouthing" games with possessive dogs, since they might react aggressively.

Following a scent
Many dogs, especially scent hounds, enjoy the mental concentration of following a scent trail. You can lay down a track for the dog by walking through grass, leaving a reward at the end.

Jogging
Healthy dogs need plenty of exercise, and training the dog to run to heel with you while you jog is both enjoyable and physically stimulating.

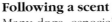

Playing with Others

Most dogs enjoy playing with other canines if they had the opportunity to do so when they were young. Females will usually play more readily than unneutered males, who are more territorial, and more prone to fighting. Initial meetings between dogs should take place on neutral territory. Do not let your dog pull on its lead: this stimulates aggression.

Body language shows dog is relaxed

Meeting on neutral territory

Arrange for your dog to meet other dogs, with each dog on a lead. Let them investigate each other, but watch for aggressive eye contact. At the first sign of aggression, turn your dog's head away and produce a favorite toy as a distraction.

Meeting through the fence

Once the dogs have successfully been introduced elsewhere, let them meet through a garden fence, or in front of your homes. Reward your dog's calm behavior.

Owner holds cat gently

Clear hand signals are used

Both dogs are on home territory

Responding to commands

Control the dog with verbal and physical commands when it is playing with other dogs. When you are ready to leave, use hand signals and verbal commands to instruct the dog to sit, then go to it and attach the lead.

Dog sits obediently

Meeting cats

Supervise first meetings between a dog and a cat. You may get scratched if you try to hold a cat that wants to flee.

Conflicts over possessions

Avoid conflicts over bones and other desirable items by either not giving them, or giving them in separate rooms. Many dogs naturally want what another dog has, even if they have an identical object, and bones and chews are the items most dogs fight over.

Dog is content for the moment

Male asserts authority by standing over female

Female behaves in subservient manner

The opposite sex

Fighting is less likely between dogs of different sexes than it is between dogs of the same sex, and of similar ages and sizes. Initial meetings should take place with both dogs on their leads.

Dog is alert but shows no sign of aggression

The same sex

Take care when dogs of the same size and sex meet. Do not permit lead tension, since this can provoke aggression. Reward the dog with verbal praise for quietly sniffing and investigating.

New Dog in the Home

Both dogs are on leads

A new dog is a potential threat to the territory of the resident dog. Do not let a new puppy jump on the older dog, since the resident dog will find this provocative. Arrange meetings in neutral territory when both dogs are relaxed, and reward the dog for its obedience in the presence of the newcomer. Feed both dogs in the same room, making sure that there is no eye contact between them. Provide each dog with its own bed, placed in a private area. Continue to greet and reward the resident dog first, and try not to change your routines.

CHAPTER FOUR

Overcoming Bad Habits

Dogs are not perfect, and even the gentlest and most obedient pet can develop unwanted habits. If your dog develops bad habits, always try to find and eliminate the cause – even though avoiding a problem is often the easiest solution and usually simpler than retraining the dog. Dogs that destroy homes when they are left alone do so not for reasons of revenge, but because they are bored, frustrated, or suffering from separation anxiety. Some bad habits, such as chasing livestock or aggression toward other dogs, are part of some dogs' normal behavior. These bad habits are difficult to overcome, but slow, repetitive, and consistent retraining is usually effective. However, you should seek professional help for the most dangerous or troubling problems, such as fear biting or aggression toward people.

Understanding and Prevention

In order to correct your dog's bad habits, it is important to understand how they first developed. Although you may find your dog's behavior unacceptable, to the dog it is simply acting naturally. When a problem develops, you should try to figure out the reason for it. Ask yourself why the behavior is unacceptable and whether the dog understands that you regard it as wrong. Try to ascertain whether the behavior can be prevented, redirected, or changed – either by yourself or by a trainer.

Acceptable natural behavior
Chewing bones, or toys that look like bones, is normal canine behavior. Chewing is a way for dogs to find out about their environment.

Object is held firmly by forepaws

Unacceptable natural behavior
Chewing a shoe covered in human scent is a natural way for a dog to behave, but it is usually unacceptable to humans. You can prevent this bad habit from forming by never giving the dog old shoes to chew. The dog will learn to restrict its chewing to allowable objects.

Hand is seen as potentially dangerous

Learned behavior
Fear of hands is learned behavior and may occur if the dog has been abused at some time. You should prevent hand shyness by never using your hands to discipline the dog.

Chewing for satisfaction
Many dogs delight in chewing objects, shredding newspaper, and even peeling wallpaper from walls. This desire to be "creative" requires acceptable outlets, such as bones to chew.

Safe toys should either be digestible or indestructible

Dog looks content after satisfying its desire to chew

Destructive behavior
Although destructive behavior is satisfying to dogs, it is unacceptable to humans. Limit the toys available to the dog to three or four that are different from other household articles. Rotate these toys and for a special treat, you can stuff a hollow rubber toy with something tasty.

BASIC CORRECTION TECHNIQUES

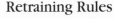

Dog recognizes that raised finger means "No"

Discipline

It is important that the dog understands what kinds of behavior you find unacceptable. You should discipline the dog only when it is actively misbehaving. Use a stern tone of voice when reprimanding the dog.

Prevention

It is always easier to prevent problems than to cure them. Apply bitter spray to objects that are attractive to dogs, such as shoes *(see page 31).*

Spray is bitter, but nontoxic

Shoe will taste unpleasant to dog

Retraining Rules

Although bad habits vary, almost all of them can be corrected by following a standard retraining program.

1 Make sure that the dog does something for you, such as sitting or lying down *(see pages 56 and 60)* before it receives verbal or physical rewards.

2 Go back to basic obedience training. Make sure that the dog sits and stays on command *(see page 56).*

3 Ensure that the dog is always under your control. Both indoors and outdoors, keep the dog on a lead or longline until you are certain that it will respond to your commands.

4 Eliminate the satisfaction that the dog obtains from its bad behavior. Sometimes this will involve mild punishment *(see page 20).*

5 Persevere with the program, and bear in mind that bad habits cannot be eliminated overnight. It may take several weeks before the problem is firmly under control.

6 For serious problems, in which injury to you, the dog, or other people is possible, you should seek professional help from a qualified dog trainer.

Confinement

If the dog chews persistently, train it to stay in a crate when it is at home alone *(see page 34).* Always provide the dog with acceptable toys to chew when it is in its crate.

Toys provide an outlet for dog's natural behavior

Assessing Temperament

It is an unfortunate fact that animal shelters experience a high rate of return. This is because many people make choices based on a dog's appearance, not its temperament. Rescued dogs are particularly prone to separation-related problems. If you are acquiring a dog more than six months old, test it for behavioral problems by carrying out as many of the following exercises as conditions and time allow. If you adopt a dog with problems, considerable time and patience will be required.

Nervousness

With the handler from the shelter holding the dog on a slack lead, quietly approach it from the front, maintaining eye contact. A relaxed dog will enjoy your approach, while a nervous dog may bark or cower.

Dog is happy with direct eye contact

Hand shyness

With the dog still on a loose lead, stroke it under its chin, and then down its back. Talk to the dog quietly as you do this. A dog that fears hands will pull away.

Dog willingly accepts being touched

Willingness to obey

Taking the lead from the handler, command the dog to sit. The dog's response will tell you whether it has had any obedience training.

Willingness to respond

If the dog does not obey, tuck it into a sit position, in order to gauge its inclination to respond to training.

Canine aggression

With the help of the handler, introduce the dog to a confident dog of the same sex. If the dog simply sniffs curiously there should be no problems with aggression toward other dogs.

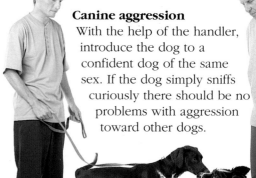

Fear of children

Holding the dog on a slack lead, introduce it to a child. The child should avoid direct eye contact with the dog. The response elicited will indicate whether the dog is nervous of children.

Dog looks anxious, but remains quiet

Additional Tests

REACTION TO CARS

Some dogs experience motion sickness or nausea when they travel in cars. If you are intending to take the dog on car journeys, test its reaction to a five-minute car ride.

Cat is at ease with dog

REACTION TO CATS

If you have a cat, introduce the dog to it very carefully. For extra safety, you can put the cat in a cat basket or cage. You should expect the dog to be curious, but a predatory response can indicate potentially serious problems.

OTHER SENSITIVITIES

Some dogs are frightened by loud noises, and others by unexpected sights such as umbrellas being put up. Be creative and test the dog in the everyday situations it will encounter in your home.

Separation anxiety

Ascertain whether the dog barks, or shows any other signs of anxiety, when it is left alone in a room for ten minutes.

Fear of strangers

Maintaining control with a slack lead, have the dog examined by a stranger. This will indicate any problems that might appear on visits to the vet or during grooming sessions.

Dog shows no fear

Possessiveness

Holding the dog by its lead, remove its food bowl. Praise the dog, then return the food. If the dog shows no aggression, it is not likely to be possessive over food. Repeat this procedure using a toy and a bone.

Lead is taut for control

Pulling on the Lead

Pulling on the lead is the most common problem experienced by dog owners. It can be caused by boredom or excitement, or it may be a manifestation of dominant behavior. You should not attempt to match your strength against the dog's by repeatedly pulling back on the lead. If your pet pulls persistently, retrain it in basic obedience commands *(see pages 56–61)* and walking to heel *(see page 70)*. Combine these basic lessons with the specific remedial techniques shown here.

THE PROBLEM

Sometimes the lead itself incites the dog to pull. It is therefore important not to use the lead as an object of force. You should try and assess why the dog pulls before attempting to correct its behavior.

THE REMEDY

1 Begin to walk with the dog on your left side, holding the lead in both hands. When the dog pulls, slide your left hand down the lead and pull back firmly.

2 When the dog is in the correct heel position, command it to sit. Start to walk again, giving the command "Heel." Repeat the procedure each time the dog pulls forward.

Hand pulls back once, gently but firmly

3 Once the dog walks quietly to heel without pulling, reward it with a food treat. Gradually increase the distance you travel, but not the time of the training sessions.

Owner gives food reward

OTHER REMEDIES

"WAIT"

Turning away
When the dog pulls, use an element of surprise – turn immediately in the opposite direction. Praise the dog when it follows you.

Lead is kept short

Hand signals
As the dog lunges forward, give the command "Wait," and put your right hand in front of its nose. Keep a firm grip on the lead with your left hand.

No hand resistance
Keeping the lead attached to the collar, loop it around your waist. Hold the lead lightly, and keep the dog in the heel position using food, a toy, or verbal commands as incentives.

Tidbit keeps dog's attention

Lead as harness
To guarantee a short lead, and to reduce tension on the dog's neck, use its lead as a harness when bringing it back to the heel position *(see page 54)*.

Other Lead Problems

CHEWING AND CLIMBING
To young and boisterous dogs, leads are exciting new toys. Such dogs sometimes chew their leads or try to climb them.

Dog chews playfully

THE REMEDY
Make the lead unpleasant to chew by spraying it with a bitter-tasting liquid *(see page 31)*. When the dog tries to chew or climb the lead, it is disciplined by the unpleasant taste, rather than by you.

Direct spray at lead, not at dog

COLLAPSING SUBMISSIVELY
While some dogs collapse because they are intimidated when brought back to the heel position, others regard it as a game, and roll over in play.

Paw is raised submissively

THE REMEDY
If the dog collapses, step backward, and use a toy to excite the dog and induce it to get up.

Toy is offered as reward

Refusing to Come

If your dog refuses to come to your call, find out the cause of its reluctance to obey before going back to recall training *(see page 58)*. Your dog may not have bonded to you; it may be bored, scavenging, or distracted by sexual opportunities; or it may have an excess of energy, or a desire to play with other dogs. Your dog may also be displaying dominant behavior, or it may be afraid of either you or the lead. You should never call your dog to something that it considers unpleasant, such as a bath.

On the scent
Dogs have a sophisticated sense of smell, and they acquire information about their environment through scenting. Allow the dog to sniff, call its name, tell it to sit, then command "Come."

Dog sniffs ground for scent messages

Natural distraction
Even if the dog understands your recall command, it might choose to disregard it in favor of a sexual investigation. Neutered dogs are less interested in sex than unaltered ones, and are more likely to come when called.

Sex-related scents are potent

Scent is sprayed below dog's nose

Scent obstruction
If the dog is an obsessive sniffer, spray perfume under its nose. This temporarily interferes with the sensitivity of the dog's scenting, so it will not be easily distracted.

Utter boredom
If the dog does not consider you to be a worthy leader, it will not respond to your recall command. You should go back to the basic commands before continuing with recall training.

Dog is bored and listless

Complete exhilaration

Young dogs tend to have a surplus of energy. If you have a young dog, make sure that it is well exercised before recalling it. If you are doubtful of the dog's compliance, keep it on an extending lead.

Tongue hangs out with exhaustion following exercise

Extra Precautions

CAUTIOUS COMMAND

Only issue the "Come" command when you can enforce it. When the dog has had thorough recall training at home, graduate to outdoor areas Initially, leave a long trailing or extending lead on the dog, to avoid grasping its collar *(see below)*, and always take food or toy rewards with you on outdoor trips.

FINAL REWARDS

Vary the play areas you take the dog to, since dogs can be obedient in one location, but not in others. Be energetic and enthusiastic when you call the dog, and praise it lavishly when it returns. At the end of the exercise period, rather than calling the dog to you, command it to sit, then go to it and put on its lead. Give the dog a reward before taking it home.

LEAD FEAR

Never discipline the dog with the lead or chastise it when it returns to you. Do not grab the dog by its collar, since it may think you are playing and avoid your grasp until you train it to accept a collar grip.

Dog shrinks from lead

Disobedience

Dogs can be temporarily distracted by an exciting activity. Attract the dog's attention by calling its name enthusiastically, then commanding it to come.

Dog ignores owner's calls

Successful scavenging

Scavenging and stealing can be more satisfying to the dog than your praise or food rewards. You should control this type of behavior with either a long lead or a muzzle.

Finding and chewing are rewarding activities

Rewarding obedience

Reinforce your recall command by holding the dog by its collar, and giving it a food treat. If necessary, use rewards such as food or a favorite toy to entice the dog back to you.

Dog eagerly receives food reward

Playtime

Allow the dog the pleasure of playing with others, but observe its behavior and give the command "Come" if the play starts to become too boisterous.

Chasing Vehicles

The desire to chase is part of normal canine behavior, although the intensity of the desire varies from breed to breed, and among individuals. The instinct is stimulated by movement, and is reinforced if other dogs join in. It is possible to control chasing behavior, but it can never be totally eliminated. You should not permit your dog to indulge in chasing, since it is a difficult problem to overcome, and can endanger its life.

THE PROBLEM

Tail is curled with excitement

Chasing cars
Chasing cars may be rewarding for the dog, but it is dangerous. The car drives away, so the dog may be satisfied, but it is also on a potentially lethal road.

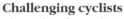

Bull Terriers are persistent chasers

Challenging cyclists
The sight of a cyclist stimulates many dogs to give chase. Because few cyclists ever stop, the dog considers the chase a success.

Water is squirted while dog is still running

POSSIBLE REMEDY

Ask a friend to cycle or drive past the dog. As the dog begins to chase, the cyclist should stop suddenly, squirt the dog with a water pistol, and say "No."

"JORDAN, SIT"

Long lead prevents dog from chasing

Cyclist goes slowly at first

REMEDIAL EXERCISE

1 Enlist the help of a friend to cycle or drive past for this exercise. As the cycle goes past slowly, command the dog to sit, holding a food reward in your hand. Make sure that the dog is under control during the exercise, using a lead or longline; it must not be given the opportunity to chase successfully.

2 Give the dog the food reward for sitting on command as the cyclist passes. Repeat the exercise until the dog reliably obeys your sit command, without attempting to chase, even as the speed of the cyclist increases. Then reward the dog with its favorite toy.

Food is used as distraction and reward

3 Repeat steps 1 and 2, using the toy as the distraction, with the cyclist traveling faster. Then progress to throwing the toy for the dog to retrieve *(see page 74)*, in the opposite direction from the cyclist, to distract the dog from chasing.

Dog concentrates on toy

Breed Predispositions

BUILT FOR SPEED

The Greyhound is a classic sight hound

Sight hounds, which are swift runners, and herding breeds, are natural chasers. Terriers are also instinctive chasers, but they often have short legs and cannot run fast.

LASTING STAMINA

Arctic breeds of dog, such as Huskies and other spitzes, are slower than sight hounds, but have tremendous stamina, and are more likely to chase over long distances.

SLOW BUT SURE

Scent hounds, like this Bloodhound, and sporting dogs, such as breeds of pointers, setters, and retrievers, are less likely to chase than other breeds.

Chasing Animals

For thousands of years of evolution, dogs survived by chasing and killing other animals. Through selective breeding, humans have diminished this instinct, but it remains intense in some breeds and individuals. Chasing is natural canine behavior, but it is also a serious problem, especially for livestock owners. One way of dealing with the problem involves training the dog to chase a safe object instead of other animals. If you are in any doubt about your ability to correct this problem, you should seek the advice of a professional dog trainer.

CHASING LIVESTOCK

Unless the dog was socialized with other animals while it was still young *(see page 19)*, you should anticipate problems when it meets potential prey. This dog stares intently at a goat, but it is on a lead and under the owner's control. Never allow a dog to walk off the lead on farmland unless you know from previous experience that it does not chase other animals. You should take similar precautions when it meets any other species for the first time.

Dog intently and provocatively "eyeballs" goat

Dog is allowed to shake and pull on toy

THE REMEDY

1 The object of this exercise is to channel the dog's chase instinct into a controllable exercise. Experiment with different toys to discover which one the dog finds most exciting. Tease the dog vigorously with the toy.

2 In a quiet location, with the dog on a longline, throw the toy, but keep another exciting toy by your side. The dog will naturally chase the thrown toy.

Longline gives owner control

Dog instinctively chases exciting object

Object has not been retrieved

"BILBO, COME"

Second toy is waved invitingly

3 Before the dog reaches the toy, call its name and command it to return to you *(see page 58)*. Be dramatic when recalling the dog and wave the second toy to entice it to return. Then play with and praise the dog.

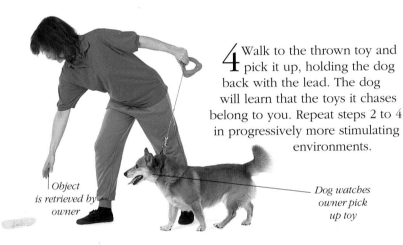

4 Walk to the thrown toy and pick it up, holding the dog back with the lead. The dog will learn that the toys it chases belong to you. Repeat steps 2 to 4 in progressively more stimulating environments.

Object is retrieved by owner

Dog watches owner pick up toy

5 Once the dog has been successfully trained not to chase an object, carry out a real retrieval exercise in the presence of livestock. Throw the toy in the opposite direction from the other animal and encourage the dog to fetch it. You will soon be able to control the dog's instinct to chase by playing exciting retrieval games.

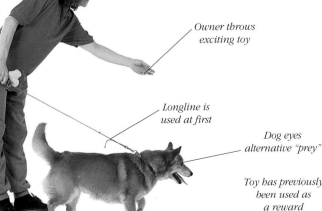

Owner throws exciting toy

Longline is used at first

Dog eyes alternative "prey"

Toy has previously been used as a reward

Dogs and Cats

GOOD FRIENDS

Dogs and cats enjoy each other's company if they are introduced to each other at an early age. Whenever possible, introduce a dog and a cat when both are about twelve weeks of age. This must be done with supervision.

If either animal is older, allow the resident to sniff the newcomer. First meetings should be supervised, and the dog should be prevented from chasing the cat.

COMPETITION

A resident animal may resent a new addition to your home and regard it as competition for food or your affection. Reduce this risk by feeding both animals at the same time on the opposite sides of a closed door, or by feeding the dog on the ground and the cat at a higher level. Reward the dog with verbal and physical praise when it behaves with curiosity but gentleness with the cat. If the dog is not predatory or dominant toward the cat, the cat will eventually be in control.

Aggression Toward Dogs

Dominant aggression is most commonly directed toward another dog of the same sex. It is seen more often in males than in females, and occurs more frequently in some breeds than in others. This form of aggression is most likely to occur when the dog is on its own territory. Some dogs are simply social misfits, but more often the problem is sex-hormone-related, or has developed because of a lack of early and continuing socialization with other dogs. This can be difficult to deal with, and you may need professional help. Neutering at a young age reduces this behavior in most male dogs.

SIGNS OF AGGRESSION

A fierce challenge

Dominantly aggressive dogs mean business. On most occasions, fighting is preceded by aggressive body posturing and growling. Unless one of the dogs backs down, a fight will ensue. During a fight, a dog is likely to bite whoever intervenes – even its owner.

Barking madly is an intimidating preliminary to an attack

Eye contact

You should intervene the moment your dog makes eye contact with a potential adversary. A raised tail and intense concentration are indicators that a fight might begin.

Between you and the dog

Some dogs will aggressively defend their owners. Standing between you and the other dog and pulling on the lead actually enhances the dog's feeling of aggression. The dog will eventually associate the feeling of straining on a lead with aggression, while it may show no aggression off the lead.

Straining on the lead provokes more aggression

Tight-lead syndrome

Although you may instinctively try to keep the dog on a short lead when aggressive behavior begins, this will often exacerbate the situation. Forcibly pulling the dog back will increase its aggression. You should turn your dog's head away so that it cannot make eye contact with the other dog.

THE REMEDY

1 Starting in a quiet environment, practice recall training with the dog *(see page 58)*. Retrain the dog on a longline or extending lead to return to you on command for a favorite toy.

Ball-on-a-rope is a tempting toy

During retraining, dog's return is ensured by using longline

2 When the dog has been retrained to come to you in a quiet area, practice the exercise in an open space with another dog in the distance. Reward the dog for not showing aggression toward the other dog. Every day, reduce the distance between the dogs, rewarding your pet for its calm behavior.

Other dog is positioned some distance away at first

Dog is kept on extending lead during training

PREVENTION

Deflect concentration
When you encounter a potentially aggressive situation, you should attract your dog's attention with its favorite toy and then issue a sit command. Always reward the dog's good behavior.

Anticipate problems
Train the dog to wear a muzzle *(see pages 33 and 55)*. The muzzle physically prevents the dog from biting and diminishes its dominance.

Dog concentrates on potential reward

Additional Information

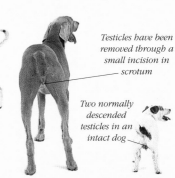

Testicles have been removed through a small incision in scrotum

Two normally descended testicles in an intact dog

MALE NEUTERING
Although spaying females is a sensible way to control unwanted pregnancies and behavior, some people have unwarranted objections to castrating dogs – a far less invasive procedure. Surgically speaking, castration is a minor operation.

Female bares her teeth aggressively

MATERNAL AGGRESSION
Female hormones heighten maternal aggression in some females. During twice-yearly periods of hormonal increase, some individuals become irritable, possessive of toys and bones, and protective of their dens. Neutering diminishes this form – but not all forms – of female aggression.

SIMILAR PROBLEMS
Dogs that are equals are more likely to fight with each other than are dogs of different size, age, or sex. Some breeds, like Dobermanns, are more prone to aggression between equals than are other breeds.

Aggression Toward People

Most dogs are content to be treated as subordinate members of the pack, and are willing to obey the commands of all members of their human family. Some dogs, however, are unwittingly taught by their owners that they are the real leaders of the pack. Leaders go through doors first, are fed first, and have their demands for comfort and affection met immediately. Once a dog thinks that it is the pack leader, it is likely to use aggression to enforce its control. You may require the services of a professional dog trainer in order to correct this behavior.

DOMINANT AGGRESSION

Dominant dog stares directly at stranger

This dog challenges an approaching person. Its aggression is based on dominance, although other dogs might act this way because they are frightened *(see page 100)*. You must determine the cause of the aggression, because the correction methods for these two problems are different.

THE REMEDY

No comforts
Making sure that the dominant dog wears a houseline at home, give the command "Off" if it climbs on the furniture.

Houseline prevents risk of bites

No risks
Using a muzzle or an adjustable head collar *(see page 33)* to ensure that the dog's mouth is closed will subdue the dog, reduce the risk of bites, and encourage it to respond to commands.

Restrained dog quietly obeys "Sit" command

Dog's plea for attention is ignored

No response
Withdraw all affection from the dog. In order to regain your attention, the dog must do something for you. Disregard the dog until it stops making demands, then command it to sit and stroke it. The dog will quickly learn that you are in control.

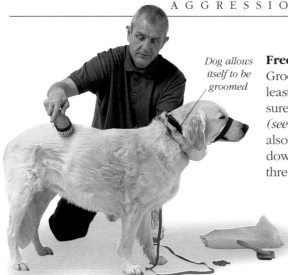

Dog allows itself to be groomed

Frequent grooming

Groom a dominant dog at least once a day, making sure that its mouth is closed *(see opposite)*. You should also put the dog in a long down at least twice a day for three weeks *(see page 64)*.

(see opposite) ... *(see page 64)*

Food is prepared but not given immediately

Dog sees that people eat first

Last to eat

In the wolf pack, the leader eats before his subordinates. Prepare the dog's food, but do not offer it until you have finished eating. Do not give the dog any food treats between meals during the weeks of retraining.

Last to leave

Do not let the dog charge out of the door in front of you. Leaders go first, and you are the leader of the pack. The dog must adjust its pace to yours.

Dog follows owner through doorway

More Control

OPEN-PLAN BED

Open-plan bedding is difficult to defend

A dominantly aggressive dog should wear a houseline even when it is resting. Make sure that the dog's sleeping area is in the open, and not in a denlike corner or other enclosed space. Dogs feel more secure in dens, and a dominant dog's confidence should not be enhanced.

FETCH EXERCISES

Carry out pick-up-and-retrieve exercises, since these help teach the dog that you are the leader. Ensure that the dog wears a houseline.

MEDICAL INTERVENTION

Dominant aggression is a potentially serious problem. Consult a trainer and your vet. If retraining is not effective, they may advise medical intervention.

ANTIANXIETY PILLS

TRANQUILIZER CAPSULES

ANTICONVULSANT TABLETS

HORMONE TABLETS

Fear Biting

Although the snap of a fearful dog's jaws may look like dominant aggression *(see page 98)*, fear biting has different causes and requires different correction. The fear-biting dog is more apprehensive and more likely to cower behind its owner's legs than an aggressive animal. The problem results from inadequate socialization in some individuals, but it can be genetic in such breeds as German Shepherd Dogs. Retraining of a fear-biting dog should be slow and cautious, and professional help is often useful.

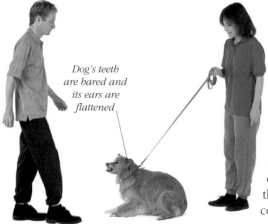

Dog's teeth are bared and its ears are flattened

FEARFUL AGGRESSION

The fear-biting dog often gives out mixed signals. The dog may cower near its owner and wag its tail submissively, but then lunge forward provocatively. Dogs with this behavioral problem usually have low self-esteem. Asserting your authority during training, as you would with a dominantly aggressive dog, only exaggerates the dog's lack of confidence.

THE REMEDY

1 You will need the help of a friend or a professional trainer. The dog should be on a long lead and should not have been fed before the exercise. Your friend should walk away, holding a food treat.

Eyes look forward

2 Allow the dog to walk toward your friend and take the food treat from the open palm. Your friend should not speak to the dog, and he should kneel with his back to it, avoiding any eye contact.

3 Carry out steps 1 and 2 several times, then repeat them with your friend turning his body slightly toward the dog. There should still be no eye contact between him and the dog.

Body is turned toward dog

4 After successful attempts at the exercise over several days, proceed to the next stage. Repeat steps 1 and 2, with your friend turning to face the dog, again kneeling down.

Intimidating eye contact is still avoided

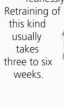

Fear of Dogs

CANINE PHOBIA

Fear of other dogs may result from lack of early experience with other canines, or from being overprotected by owners; or it could be a consequence of having previously been frightened or bitten.

THE REMEDY

With the help of a friend who has a placid dog, go for a walk in an open space and find the distance at which your dog does not show fear in the presence of the other dog. Reward the dog with food treats and affection when it displays relaxed behavior. Every day, reduce the distance separating the two dogs until your dog walks fearlessly beside the other. Retraining of this kind usually takes three to six weeks.

Snack is offered to dog

5 Now walk the dog toward your friend, who should be stationary. Avoiding eye contact with the dog, he should face it, offer the food treat, and step back. If the dog becomes fearful at this stage, go back to the previous stage and repeat it.

6 Walk toward your friend, and as the dog takes the treat, praise it and stroke it along its body. Your friend should still be avoiding eye contact with the dog, but he can talk quietly to you. It will probably take several weeks to reach this stage.

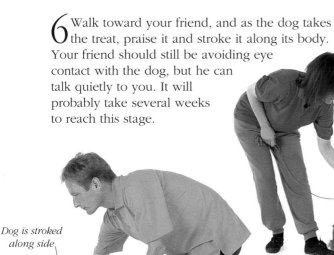

Dog confidently takes food while being touched

Dog is stroked along side

7 Once the dog behaves confidently while you stroke it and your associate gives it a food treat, he should give the snack while stroking the dog's side. After repeating this exercise many times, make a subtle change. Still avoiding eye contact, your assistant should stroke the dog before giving the food reward.

Guarding

Possessiveness is a behavioral problem that is most frequently encountered in dominant dogs. Pack leaders are more likely to decide that they own toys, food bowls, and resting places than are more submissive dogs, but there are also breed predispositions. For example, terriers are possessive of food, toys, and rest areas. Avoid confrontations with a possessive dog by not giving it toys and not allowing it to sit on your furniture. You should treat problems by withdrawing affection, reteaching basic commands, and keeping your dog on a training lead.

GUARDING FOOD

Dog threatens with a growl

This dog growls possessively and dominantly as its owner approaches its food bowl. The dog feels that it is pack leader, and leaders protect their possessions – they do not share. Both males and females may indulge in guarding behavior. If you back down when the dog growls, it will learn that this behavior is effective and will be encouraged to use it more frequently.

THE REMEDY

1 When carrying out this exercise, make sure that the dog is held on a training lead by a friend or a member of the family. Do not feed the dog before the exercise. Offer the dog a bowl containing a small amount of bland food, such as rice, instead of a full bowl of tasty food. Let the dog sniff the food.

Food bowl contains only rice

2 With the dog watching, introduce a small amount of tastier food. Repeat this exercise every time you feed the dog, and after several days it will welcome your visit to its food bowl.

Dog watches as owner adds food

Tasty food is put into bowl

GUARDING FURNITURE

Dominant dogs choose their resting places. This dog has chosen a chair and is guarding it, along with a toy that it considers its own. You should never pull on a dominant dog's collar, since it may try to bite.

THE REMEDY

Keep the dog's training lead on throughout the day; this will ensure that you have complete control. Induce the dog to leave the chair by commanding "Off," and offering a food reward. A slight jerk on the lead may be necessary at first.

"OFF"

Food is used as inducement for dog to jump down

Guarding the Family

Stranger approaches owner

Dog growls protectively

OWNER-POSSESSIVE
Although humans appreciate the security that dogs provide, some dogs become extremely possessive of their owners – especially if they are of the opposite sex.

THE REMEDY
If the dog becomes too possessive, keep it on a lead so that you are able to control it when visitors arrive. Leave a food snack near the front door for a friend to bring in. As the visitor enters, command the dog to sit and stay. Instruct the visitor to avoid eye contact with the dog and to crouch down and offer the food reward.

Dog stops growling in order to take treat

GUARDING TOYS

Some dogs will guard toys and refuse to relinquish them. You should avoid tug-of-war games with these dogs, since they always play to win.

THE REMEDY

1 With a tasty treat in one hand and a toy in the other, encourage the dog to take the toy.

2 Issue the command "Give," and when the dog releases the toy, reward it by saying "Good dog" and giving the food. Repeat the exercise immediately by giving the toy back to the dog, then commanding "Give" again.

Dog is rewarded with snack

Rivalry Between Dogs

Humans are not the only species to experience emotions – dogs have them, too. Jealousy and rivalry are most likely to occur in dogs of the same sex, size, age, and temperament. They may squabble over bones, sleeping areas, or for their owner's attention. Dogs cannot share certain personal items, so each dog should have its own bed and food bowl – although a water bowl can be shared. Some dominant breeds experience more sibling rivalry than other breeds. Neutering the underdog may be necessary to increase the difference between two resident male dogs.

SIBLING RIVALRY

Arguing over possessions

Bones are the objects most likely to provoke arguments between littermates. Avoid potential problems either by not giving bones at all or by giving them in separate rooms. It does not matter how many bones you offer; one dog will always want the other's bone.

Dog growls aggressively because it wants the other dog's bone

Dogs eat without making eye contact

Avoid eye contact

Reduce rivalry by feeding your dogs together, but ensure that they face in opposite directions. Each dog will learn that it will receive a food reward if it eats with the other without fighting. Always put the dominant dog's bowl down first.

Mutual rewards

If the dogs have similar personalities, and there are no clear indications that one is dominant, issue joint commands such as "Sit," and reward both dogs at the same time. They will learn to be obedient in each other's presence.

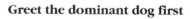

Less dominant dog waits to be greeted by owner

Mutual rewards are given without provoking jealousy

Dominant dog is greeted and rewarded

Greet the dominant dog first

There is no democracy in the canine world. If the dogs give you indications about which one is top dog, you should acknowledge their relationship by greeting the leader first. This reduces the dominant dog's need to show its authority.

J E A L O U S Y

Introducing a puppy

Although most dogs eventually enjoy the introduction of another dog into the home, there may be some jealousy at first. Reduce problems by adhering to your routines as much as possible. Give the resident dog plenty of attention in the presence of the new arrival; it will soon associate the puppy with pleasurable activities.

Resident dog receives attention

Puppy is disregarded

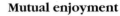

Mutual enjoyment

Feed the resident dog and the new puppy together, but make sure that there is no eye contact between them. Feed the older dog as often as the puppy, but without increasing the total quantity of its food.

Dog gets no response from owner

Gentle disregard

When the new puppy is absent, ignore the older dog. It will learn to associate the presence of the puppy with increased attention from you.

Allow escape

Puppies can be exhilarating but also exasperating. The resident dog may become tired of the constant pestering from the youngster. Set up a barrier so that the older dog can escape from the puppy's demands.

Puppy is restricted by barrier

Personal Space

All dogs need their own private territories, somewhere they can go when they are tired or when they want to be alone. Provide each dog with the security of its own bed. You should not allow one dog to use the other's bed, since this can lead to disputes. Each bed should contain comfortable, clean, washable bedding.

Dog is content in its own bed

Problems with Sex

Excessive canine sexual behavior is perfectly natural, but it can sometimes be annoying. The sex-related problems of urine marking, wandering, territory guarding, fighting with other dogs, and overprotectiveness occur most frequently in male dogs and are easiest to control in neutered animals. Breeding a dog so that it can experience sex is counterproductive, since it may result in excessive sexual behavior later in the dog's life. Neutering females generally has little effect on behavior, although it can increase dominant behavior in naturally dominant bitches. However, simple sexual activity in both sexes can be controlled through careful training.

SEXUAL SUBSTITUTE

Dog grasps owner's leg

Mounting behavior is a part of the canine social structure. In addition to its obvious role in reproduction, it is also a sign of dominance. Males and females may both attempt to mount submissive individuals. If you allow a puppy to mount limbs, the behavior will be difficult to correct in adulthood.

THE REMEDY

Oversexed dog should wear lead or houseline at home during retraining

1 Every time the dog tries to mount a person's arm or leg, say "No," remove it using the lead, and isolate it for one minute. When the dog is oversexed, it finds any physical contact – even a reprimand – potentially gratifying, so avoid touching it.

2 Isolation is a symbolic gesture and should only be carried out for very short periods of time. After one minute, allow the dog back into your company, but ignore it.

Dog receives no attention from owner

3 After disregarding the dog for a few minutes, command it to sit, give it a reward, and play with it. The fact that the dog has mounted your leg indicates that it is in need of physical and mental stimulation. You should make sure that the dog receives enough exercise.

Tug toy may worsen the problem

MOUNTING OBJECTS

Dog clasps rug and thrusts with pelvis

If a dog is frustrated in its attempt to mount dogs and people, it may turn to furry toys, cushions, or rugs. This behavior is perfectly normal, but it can be damaging to articles and offensive to some people.

THE REMEDY

As the dog thrusts on the rug, command "Off" and squirt it with a water pistol. Most dogs find the water spray disconcerting. You should acknowledge that the dog is bored and frustrated and provide it with mental and physical activity.

Unexpected water spray diverts dog's attention

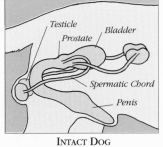

MOUNTING VISITORS

Some dogs will mount a visitor's limbs simply to get attention. Others will do so because they have learned that they are not allowed to indulge in the activity with members of the family.

Dog pants with excitement

THE REMEDY

Repeat the exercises of isolation, disregard, and command *(see opposite)*. You could avoid embarrassment by keeping the dog in another room whenever you have visitors, but most people want their dog to be part of their household activities.

Alternatively, keep the dog on a lead and instruct your visitor not to excite or arouse it.

Neutering

If the dog is not to be used for breeding, and if it has any bad habits related to sex hormone, discuss with your vet the advantages of having the dog neutered. Neutering does not alter a dog's basic personality; it simply lessens the likelihood of sex-related problems.

Testicle · Prostate · Bladder · Spermatic Chord · Penis

INTACT DOG

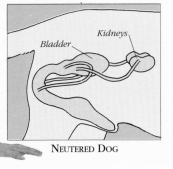

Bladder · Kidneys

NEUTERED DOG

Problems in Cars

Some dogs enjoy car travel, both because they find the journeys exciting, and because car trips often end in exercise and meetings with other dogs. Some dogs hate traveling in cars because of the uncontrolled motion, resulting in nausea. Try to take your dog on frequent, short trips so that it becomes accustomed to the car. If your dog dribbles or experiences car sickness, do not feed it before a trip, and protect the car with newspapers or old towels. Reprimand your dog if it shows signs of defending the car as its own territory.

Beginning the journey
Entice the dog into the car with food (if it does not suffer from nausea) or a toy, but do not overexcite the dog before you embark on a trip.

Dog waits before jumping into car

No nausea-induced dribbling

Dog pants contentedly

Newspaper protects car seat

A second home
At first, provide the dog with a toy and a bowl of food in the car, so that it associates car travel with enjoyable activities. Remove the food bowl before the journey.

Excessive barking

If the dog is unruly in the car and barks excessively, someone should sit with it and command it to be quiet when necessary *(see page 66).*

As dog howls, owner firmly commands "Quiet"

Destructive digging

Left on its own in the car, the dog may dig into and chew the interior. Spray the seat belts and upholstery with a non-toxic, bitter substance, and provide the dog with an attractive chew toy.

Dog's nails can destroy seat fabric

Sunblind

A sunblind on the car window will keep the sun off the dog. It is also useful for calming down excitable dogs, since it obscures their view and makes the ride less stimulating.

Sunblind can be easily attached to car window

Further Precautions

Crates fit best in station wagons and hatch-backs

Dog is content and relaxed

TRANSPORTATION CRATE

Crate-trained dogs can undertake car journeys in a transportation crate. In addition to offering safety, a crate will eliminate any destructive activity. The dog will feel secure and relaxed, but you should also provide it with a stimulating toy.

SIMPLE CONTROL

Try muzzling the dog to prevent barking and destructive behavior. Tying its lead to the seatbelt anchor will also help, since it will prevent the dog from moving around too much. Better yet, use a seatbelt harness designed to limit a dog's movement, prevent it from distracting the driver, and reduce the risk of it being injured in an accident.

CARS CAN KILL

Never leave the dog unattended in a car in warm weather; even parking in the shade and leaving a window partly open is not safe. Dogs have poor control of their body temperatures and can suffer potentially fatal heatstroke as a result of overheating. Even during cold weather, you should not leave the dog alone in a car with the heater on.

PROVIDING REFRESHMENT

Make sure that you have a container of water in the car, especially during long journeys. You should stop every few hours to allow the dog to drink and relieve itself.

Nervousness

Nervous behavior is most common in small breeds and in dogs that were isolated when they were young. However, it also occurs unexpectedly in many other dogs, for a variety of reasons. Fear of noises such as backfiring cars, thunder, or fireworks can develop – even in non-reactive breeds such as retrievers. Some dogs become frightened when they see moving objects they do not recognize, such as skateboards or strollers. Other dogs are afraid of people on crutches or in wheelchairs, and although physical abuse may be the reason why a dog is afraid of hands, in most such cases there is no history of abuse.

FEER OF NOISES

On hearing loud noises like thunder, many dogs become apprehensive and try to hide. An owner's natural reaction is to comfort the nervous dog and distract it from the source of the fear. However, this can exaggerate the dog's fearful response, since it learns that when it behaves nervously it is rewarded with contact from its owner, soothing words, and even food.

Dog has fearful expression

Tail hangs limp and tucks under

THE REMEDY

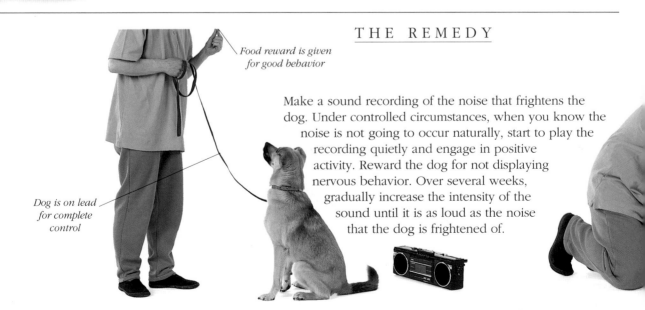

Food reward is given for good behavior

Dog is on lead for complete control

Make a sound recording of the noise that frightens the dog. Under controlled circumstances, when you know the noise is not going to occur naturally, start to play the recording quietly and engage in positive activity. Reward the dog for not displaying nervous behavior. Over several weeks, gradually increase the intensity of the sound until it is as loud as the noise that the dog is frightened of.

FEAR OF OBJECTS

Dogs are sometimes afraid of unfamiliar objects, especially those that move. Dogs that live in families with no children are often afraid of strollers and they may cower or try to run when they see one.

THE REMEDY

1 Place a tasty snack on the floor near the stroller. Do not feed the dog before the exercise, so that it will be hungry. Move treats closer to the stroller, and after several sessions the dog should put its head under the stroller to eat them.

Tidbit is placed under stroller

Dog eats from bowl

2 Once the dog willingly takes tidbits from under the stroller, graduate to placing its food bowl there. During corrective training, move the stroller occasionally and reward the dog for showing no fear.

FEAR OF HANDS

Nervous dogs often experience conflicts; they want to greet people but are afraid of hands, so they shy away.

There is a look of trepidation in dog's eyes

THE REMEDY

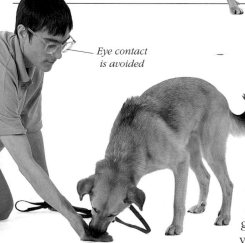

Eye contact is avoided

1 Place your palm containing a food treat on the ground in front of the dog. If you think the dog could bite, follow the remedy suggested for fear-biting dogs *(see page 100).*

2 Once the dog consistently and willingly takes the food from the ground, reduce the distance between you and the dog and move to its side.

Submissive Behavior

SUBMISSIVE URINATION

Very nervous dogs roll over submissively, and even urinate, when presented with frightening demands or situations. If the dog behaves this way during training, you are being too forceful. Do not pet or touch the dog, since this could intimidate it further.

Urination is a sign of abject submission

THE REMEDY

You should get down to the dog's level, in order to restore its confidence. Then entice the dog to get up, using a favorite toy. Playing fetch enables the dog to leave its submissive position without being physically handled by you, which can make it feel even more submissive. If the dog rolls over and urinates when you greet it, ignore it until it calms down.

Rolling over is submissive play activity

Boredom

Dogs are gregarious social animals, and their senses, minds, and bodies need stimulation. If you return home to scenes of canine destruction, do not assume that your pet has displayed this behavior as revenge for being left alone.
Dogs are incapable of carrying out premeditated crimes against property. Howling, digging, destroying, jumping, and rhythmically pacing back and forth are all signs of anxiety. You can prevent problems associated with boredom by providing natural outlets for your dog's physical and mental needs.

SEPARATION ANXIETY

Mouth is raised to produce a howl

Digging to escape
While some dogs dig to bury bones, and others to create cool pits to lie in, many dig simply out of frustration.

Digging requires concentration and dexterity

Howling for attention
Wolf cubs howl to attract the attention of their mothers. In the same way, the bored, frustrated, and understimulated dog barks or howls to gain its owner's attention when it is left alone.

Shaking rug vigorously is emotionally rewarding

Rhythmic jumping
Left in a yard, a bored dog may amuse itself by jumping to look over the fence. Separation anxiety causes some dogs to pace back and forth, urine mark, howl, and dig.

Ears point forwards eagerly

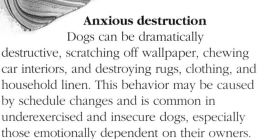

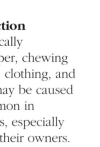

Anxious destruction
Dogs can be dramatically destructive, scratching off wallpaper, chewing car interiors, and destroying rugs, clothing, and household linen. This behavior may be caused by schedule changes and is common in underexercised and insecure dogs, especially those emotionally dependent on their owners.

PREVENTING PROBLEMS

Using the senses
Before leaving the dog alone, give it plenty of mental and physical exercise. Exhausted dogs are less likely to bark, dig, and destroy than those with excess energy.

Dog sniffs for any new smells

Meeting other dogs
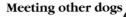
You should not isolate a dog from other canines. Arrange controlled meetings to ensure that the dog is well socialized with others.

Dog is apprehensive at first

Playing games
When you leave the dog alone, give it a toy that it is obsessed with. Rubbing the toy in your hands to cover it with your scent makes the dog feel more secure.

Chewing a toy is a rewarding activity

Off to work
Do not leave dogs at home alone for more than 8-10 hours, since they enjoy activity. If you can, take the dog to your workplace, since this will reduce boredom.

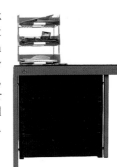

Dog has its own personal space

A helping hand
If you must leave the dog alone for long periods, prevent boredom-related problems from developing by employing a professional dog walker. Alternatively, enlist the services of a friend who can exercise the dog frequently.

All dogs are walked on leads

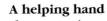

Further Prevention

PLANNING AHEAD

Check the dog's behavior by leaving it alone in a room with a toy. After a few minutes, go back into the room and praise the dog for not showing signs of boredom, such as barking, pacing, or digging at the door. Repeat this exercise in different rooms and over varying periods of time, until the dog can be left alone without exhibiting any signs of anxiety.

QUIET FAREWELL

Always leave quietly. Drawing the curtains and leaving a radio or television on will mask distracting outdoor noises. It is important to remember that even well-behaved dogs can have separation problems in new homes.

Cures for Boredom

You will find it extremely difficult to eliminate boredom-related problems unless you simultaneously eliminate the causes. Give your dog the opportunity to exercise, explore, sniff, scent, and urine mark. Increase the self-confidence of dogs that fear being left alone. Consider neutering if your male dog's barking, digging, escaping, or destroying is sex-related. Only when the cause is removed will you be in a position to retrain your pet to overcome its antisocial behavior. It is important to remember that your dog's behavior is a result of anxiety and frustration, and not a means of revenge.

HOWLING

Command training

If the dog persistently barks and howls when left alone, train it to respond to the "Quiet" command *(see page 66)*, then set up mock departures. Attract the dog's attention, command it to be quiet, and stand outside the front door. If the dog barks, drop a tin tray or throw a bunch of keys at the door in order to startle it. Return and praise the dog when it is quiet, then leave again. This exercise takes time and patience.

"QUIET"

Owner gives visual command

Eye contact is maintained

Dog has been commanded to sit

DIGGING

Rest follows feeding

Dogs are less likely to be active on full stomachs than on empty ones, so they will indulge less in digging behavior if they have been fed. If the dog is left alone during the day, feed it in the morning or twice daily.

Digging is instinctive behavior

Large meal can reduce desire for physical activity

Creative activity

Constructively redirect the dog's natural instinct to dig in flower beds or on the lawn by providing it with its own sand pit.

JUMPING

Roadblock
Prevent the dog from jumping up at the garden fence by placing chicken wire on bricks along the base. Make sure that the gauge of the wire is too small for the dog's feet to slip through. The wire will make digging and jumping difficult for the dog.

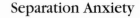

Wire provides insecure footing

Use empty tin cans on a rope

Dog sees obstacle and is reluctant to jump

Separation Anxiety
Dogs that lack confidence – particularly individuals that have been through animal shelters – are most likely to bark, dig, and destroy when left alone. These insecure animals need gentle handling, and their anxiety-related activities take time to cure. Gradually, over a period of many weeks, increase the periods of separation, always leaving the dog with a toy that you have rubbed in your hands. Discipline the dog only if you see it misbehaving – never after. Poor timing on your part will confuse the dog further.

Anxious dog cowers apprehensively when left alone

Noisy intervention
String several tin cans on a rope, about 3 feet (1 m) above the ground and about 12 inches (30 cm) from the fence. If the dog jumps and hits the string, the noise of the rattling tin cans will function as instant discipline.

CHEWING

Controlled environment
When leaving home, put the dog in its own crate with a favorite toy *(see page 34)*. You could also apply taste deterrent *(see page 31)* to the areas that the dog regularly chews.

Dog is content to chew toys while confined to crate

Physical activity
Dogs need physical activity, and the best way to reduce the problems associated with boredom is to give them daily exercise.

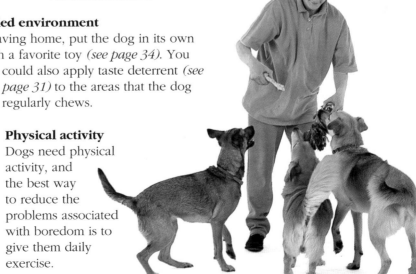

Jumping Up

Apuppy greets its mother by jumping up to lick her face. Dogs, especially adolescents between six and eighteen months old, sometimes try to do the same to humans. Excitement usually triggers this activity. Labrador Retrievers and poodles tend to jump up for affection, while dominant breeds do so to show their dominance. Do not encourage your dog's natural inclination to jump up by slapping your thighs and raising your voice when you return home. Tell children to keep their hands by their sides. If you behave calmly, your dog is also more likely to do so.

JUMPING EXCITEDLY

Dog looks directly into owner's eyes

Jumping occurs most frequently when dogs are excited. Coming home, picking up the dog's lead, or the arrival of a visitor can all stimulate jumping up. Although often an activity of young dogs, this is also the behavior of understimulated individuals. Reduce the likelihood of your dog behaving this way by ensuring that it is frequently exercised.

THE REMEDY

Dogs of this size can knock people over

Owner avoids stimulating eye contact

Owner uses visual as well as verbal command

1 You should begin to correct jumping behavior by reinforcing the dog's obedience to the "Sit" and "Stay" commands *(see page 56)*. Rather than using a negative command such as "Off," enter the room and command the dog to sit. Do not raise your voice or wave your arms, since both activities stimulate the dog.

2 Reward the dog when it sits on command, but avoid stroking the top of its head, since it may try to lick your face. Instead, crouch down to the dog's level and stroke it briskly along its flanks or under its chin. Praise the dog for its quiet behavior. Practice this exercise until the dog no longer jumps up.

CANINE MISSILE

Dog leaps with excitement

While some dogs simply jump up to lick their owners' faces, others launch themselves through the air toward people. This is normal play activity between dogs, but it is potentially dangerous to people.

THE REMEDY

You should ignore the flamboyant greeting and, avoiding eye contact, walk past the dog. When the dog's feet are back on the ground, command it to sit, then get down to its level. Praise the dog's obedience.

JUMPING UP ON VISITORS

1 If the dog persistently jumps up on visitors when they arrive, put on its lead before opening the front door. Give the command "Sit."

2 Ask a friend to bring food rewards for the dog on the next visit. The dog should receive a reward from the visitor upon sitting obediently after his arrival.

Additional Information

MEETING CHILDREN

Dog obeys owner's commands

Child quietly greets dog

Some dogs are more inclined to jump up on children than on adults, because children's faces are closer, and they often act in a more excited manner. Introduce the dog to a child under controlled conditions, with the dog on a lead. Instruct the child not to raise her arms to her face but to keep them by her sides. Reward the dog for not jumping up.

BEGGING ATTENTION

Some dogs – especially small breeds – jump up, bark, whine, or lick, in order to attract attention or to beg for food. This is canine bad manners, and you should not allow a dog to do this. Never feed the dog from the table and do not respond to its demands. If you respond, the dog will learn that the behavior works. Reduce the dog's dependence on you by making sure that other members of the family, as well as friends, play with it and feed it.

FORCEFUL CONTROL

Always use positive methods to control the dog's behavior. You should never knee the dog in its chest, step on its hind feet, or squeeze its forepaws when it jumps up. You can control the dog's behavior with common sense. Be firm, but not angry.

Excited Behavior

Dogs sometimes adopt frenzied behavioral patterns when excited. They bark hysterically, chase their tails, chew stones, compulsively groom themselves, or demand to be picked up. Consult your vet to ensure that the hysterical behavior is not caused by a medical condition. With that assurance, you should proceed with basic retraining.

EXCESSIVE BARKING

Many dogs act like canine alarms – barking when they hear unexpected noises. Some dogs, however, especially terriers, poodles, and Lhasa Apsos, become chronically excessive barkers unless they are taught to control their behavior. The barking often becomes rhythmic, and may stop only momentarily on a command from the owner. To the hysterical dog, your shouting "Quiet" appears to be an attempt to join in.

THE REMEDY

Voice control
Go back to teaching the "Speak" and "Quiet" commands *(see page 66)*, in controlled situations. Enlist the services of a friend, who can ring your doorbell while you practice the exercise.

Owner gives food reward when dog is quiet

Mild punishment
Dramatic gestures are sometimes necessary. As the dog barks, squirt a nontoxic, nonirritating, but unpleasant-tasting substance into its mouth, taking care to avoid its eyes.

TAIL CHASING

When highly excited, some dogs, especially Bull Terriers, chase their tails. Although there is a strong genetic component to the behavior, the activity is self-rewarding and increases in frequency unless it is stopped.

Dog twirls around until it catches its tail

THE REMEDY

Divert the tail chaser's attention by offering another reward. Command the dog to sit, and when it obeys, reward it with a chew toy or food snack. Seek veterinary advice if the problem persists.

Dog concentrates on owner's new reward

DEMANDING ATTENTION

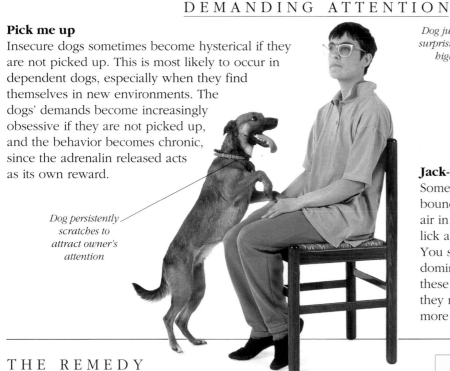

Pick me up

Insecure dogs sometimes become hysterical if they are not picked up. This is most likely to occur in dependent dogs, especially when they find themselves in new environments. The dogs' demands become increasingly obsessive if they are not picked up, and the behavior becomes chronic, since the adrenalin released acts as its own reward.

Dog persistently scratches to attract owner's attention

Dog jumps surprisingly high

Jack-in-the-box

Some dogs repetitively bounce high in the air in an attempt to lick a human face. You should not be domineering with these dogs, since they need to gain more self-esteem.

THE REMEDY

1 If the dog persistently and obsessively jumps up or scratches you with its paws, quietly leave the room. The dog will be surprised by your sudden departure.

Dog is startled into being quiet

Dog now listens to and obeys owner

2 A minute later, and while the dog is still calm, return and reassert control over the dog by commanding it to sit. You should always reward the dog's good behavior.

Compulsive Behavior

BARKING

Not all barking is compulsive; most barking is, in fact, normal and natural. Dogs bark greetings to us and to other dogs. They also have alarm barks, threat barks, and communal barks. Only uncontrolled or excessive barking is wrong. If the dog is barking excessively and will not stop, hold it by the scruff of the neck, obtain direct eye contact, give it a quick, firm shake, and say "Quiet."

LICKING

Obsessive licking of the forepaws can be a grooming disorder, similar to human grooming disorders, such as obsessive hand washing. Consult your vet, who might want to use specific drugs to control this activity. The problem is particularly common in Labrador Retrievers and Dobermanns.

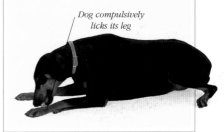

Dog compulsively licks its leg

Food Problems

From the time your dog enters your home, train it to eat only from its own bowl. Feeding the dog after the people have eaten helps to teach it to obey, since it learns that humans are more dominant than dogs. Do not leave food in accessible places or feed the dog from the dining table, and make sure that your garbage can has a secure lid. If eating problems do develop, they are not usually difficult to overcome.

STEALING FOOD

It is instinctive for dogs to look for food, and rewarding for them to find something tasty and to eat it. What humans consider garbage is often delightful to a dog.

THE REMEDY

1 If the dog scavenges in the garbage, set up situations that will entice it to carry out a raid in your presence. As the dog does this, firmly give the command "Leave," so that it understands that the activity is not permitted.

Obedient dog willingly obeys command

2 Put the lid firmly on the can. Then make the garbage less enticing by spraying the can with a nontoxic, bitter-tasting substance *(see page 31)*. Let the dog investigate the sprayed can. For this method to be effective, the unpleasant taste of the can must be greater than the reward of a raid.

This is a harmless but bitter-tasting spray

No attractive garbage is visible

BEGGING

Paw is used to attract owner's attention

Dogs that come to the table and beg for food can be a real nuisance. Giving an occasional treat from the table is actually worse than responding to the dog every time you sit down to a meal. Constant habits are easier to correct than those that occur occasionally.

THE REMEDY

1 Train the dog to take food only when permitted. Command it to sit while you prepare its food – away from the table.

Dog waits until command to take food is given

2 Put the food on the floor, but keep the dog in the sit position until you release it with the command "Take it" or "Okay."

"Disgusting" Habits

EATING ANIMAL DROPPINGS
This is a disgusting habit to us, but animal droppings can be genuinely nourishing to dogs. Scavenging herbivore droppings from horses, rabbits, and deer is natural behavior for some dogs – especially Labrador Retrievers and Golden Retrievers. Use standard obedience training to overcome this habit. If you see the dog looking with interest at an animal dropping, give the command "No." If the dog picks it up, give the command "Drop."

EATING DOG DROPPINGS
Eating its own or other dog droppings is a more dangerous habit than the one above. The dog can pick up intestinal parasites; it can also create a bacterial overgrowth condition in its intestines, resulting in chronic diarrhea. Always clean up after the dog, but to help eliminate the behavior, leave a recently passed stool and taint it with Tabasco sauce.

Dog will find peppery sauce unpleasant

REFUSING FOOD

Dog refuses to eat new variety of food

Some dogs will refuse to eat the food they are offered. This is common among toy breeds, but also occurs in large, lean breeds, such as the Saluki. Dogs can go without food for longer periods than humans.

THE REMEDY

FULL BOWL   SMALLER QUANTITY   EVEN SMALLER QUANTITY   SMALLER QUANTITY AGAIN   FRESH WATER

A healthy dog will not starve if food is present. Unless your vet advises against it, leave food for ten minutes, then remove any uneaten food. Repeat the exercise daily with smaller amounts, until the food is eaten.

Effective Training

If you want to be an effective trainer, your dog must think of you as leader of the pack. If a dog decides what and when it wants to be fed, where it wants to sleep, or when it wants to be picked up, and you respond, then even the most naturally submissive dog will soon believe that it is the dominant member of the household.

Your dog will pay attention to you only if it respects you. If you keep a record of how you behave with your dog, it will help you discover whether or not you have laid the groundwork for effective dog training. Help in training your dog is always available. Contact your local veterinary clinic for details of classes in your area.

PROFESSIONAL HELP

Puppy socialization classes
Open to owners and puppies under 16 weeks old, these weekly classes are an ideal method of introducing young dogs to other puppies and to people. Puppy parties provide a firm foundation for more formal training.

Basic obedience classes
These classes are open to older dogs, but also to puppies that

have not attended socialization classes. They are usually held by experienced dog trainers, and teach both you and your dog the basics of canine obedience.

Advanced training classes
Although basic training is perfectly adequate for most dogs, advanced training gives you more refined control of your pet. By introducing both you and your dog to the enjoyment of canine agility, tracking, special activities, games, and other dog sports, advanced training helps develop the full potential of the partnership between you and your canine companion.

Kennel training
Some kennels offer residential training courses for dogs, where your dog is trained in your absence. Although residential training can be useful for specific and specialized work, it is always best if you and your dog are able to train together.

Personal training
Some behavioral problems, for example certain forms of aggression or livestock chasing, are so serious that they warrant the help of a personal trainer. Your vet should be able to suggest someone.

Veterinary help
Unless you are a serious and responsible breeder, you should neuter your dog. Early neutering reduces, or even eliminates, the risk of mammary tumors and womb infection in females, and prostate problems and perianal tumors in males. Neutered dogs also tend to be most responsive to training. If your dog is not behaving normally, or if behavioral problems develop, consult your vet. Changed behavior might be a sign of illness, and your vet may suggest using medication for certain behavioral disorders at the same time as you work on modifying the dog's behavior.

TRAINING RECORD

Where did you acquire your dog?		Breeder/Friend		Advertisement/Shelter/Pet store
How old was your dog when you acquired it?		Under 26 weeks		Over 26 weeks
Has your female dog been neutered?		No		Yes
Has your male dog been neutered?		Yes		No
Have you previously owned a dog?		Yes		No
When is your dog fed?		Set times		On demand
Does your dog eat after you?		Yes		No
When does your dog relieve itself?		Set times		On demand
Where does your dog sleep?		Kitchen/Outdoors		Bedroom/On bed
How often is your dog groomed?		Frequently		Infrequently
How does your dog react to grooming?		Dog is willing		Dog is unwilling
When is your dog exercised?		Set times		On demand
How long is the exercise period?		More than 1 hour/day		Less than 1 hour/day
Do you have off-lead control?		Yes		No
Where are the dog's toys kept?		In toy box		On floor
How often does your dog play with other dogs?		Frequently		Infrequently
How often does your dog play with other people?		Frequently		Infrequently
How often is your dog left at home alone?		Infrequently		Frequently
How often does your dog have special playtime with you?		Frequently		Infrequently

If your answers to these questions are mainly in the first column, you are well on your way to effective dog training. If most of your answers are in the second column, you will benefit from professional advice from an experienced dog handler.

Index